MANLY HEALTH AND TRAINING

WITH OFF-HAND HINTS TOWARD THEIR CONDITIONS

BY WALT WHITMAN

First Published in Serial form in The New York Atlas - 1858

NEW AMERICAN EDITION
EDITED BY EVAN ROFHEART

FIRST EDITION

PUBLISHED by
ENLIGHTENMENT PRESS
NEW YORK CITY
2016

PREFACE

BY EVAN ROFHEART

Walt Whitman, an icon of the original American Transcendentalists, wrote Manly Health and Training, a decidedly non-transcendentalist manifesto in 1858. As was his style he wrote it using one of his common pen names, Mose Velsor. It was published in serial form by the newspaper The New York Atlas, in approximately thirteen weekly instalments.

In this edition, I have chosen to create a proper book that retains all of the original material from The New York Atlas serial, but that allows the purity of the ideas to be presented. This is the First Edition of Manly Health, in book form, edited to correct the obvious typos and spelling errors of the newspaper typesetter.

By the politically correct standards of today, it is unlikely that it would have seen the light of day. In many respects, Manly Health is very American individualist guide to life. Whitman touches on many things, food, alcohol, sex, boxing, bathing, footwear and just about anything else he felt warranted inclusion.

In an interview in the New York Times, Ed Folsom, a professor of English at the University of Iowa and Whitman scholar, speaking about Manly Health said, "One of Whitman's core beliefs was that the body was the basis of democracy." He continues, Manly Health "...is a hymn to the male body, as well as a guide to taking care of what he saw as the most vital unit of democratic living."

Manly Health is an important window into mid-1800s North-Eastern America. I am pleased to be making this valuable addition to the body of Walt Whitman's work available.

INTRODUCTION

To the 1858 Newspaper Serialization

TO YOU WHOSE eye is arrested by the above headlines, and whom we hope to make a companion to the end of our series—to every man, rich or poor, worker or idler—to all ages of life, from the beginning to the end of it—certainly nothing comes closer home, or is, without any intermission, a topic of more controlling interest, than this we are going to present, through a few articles, some plain and we hope sensible hints toward the furtherance of—a sound and steady condition of manly health. We will not make any apology for devoting a portion of our columns to the discussion of this subject; nor, indeed, do we think it much more than necessary to state our theme, to be quite certain that we shall have an eager and multitudinous audience.

Manly health! Is there not a kind of charm—a fascinating magic in the words? We fancy we see the look with which the phrase is met by many a young man, strong, alert, vigorous, whose mind has always felt, but never formed in words, the ambition to attain to the perfection of his bodily powers—has realized to himself that all other goods of existence would hardly be goods, in comparison with a perfect body, perfect blood—no morbid humours, no weakness, no impotency or deficiency or bad stuff in him; but all running over with animation and ardour, all marked by herculean strength, suppleness, a clear complexion, and the rich results (which follow such causes) of a laughing voice, a merry song morn and night, a sparkling eye, and an ever-happy soul! To such a young man—to all who read these lines—let us, with rapid pen, sketch some of the requisites toward this condition of sound health we talk of—a condition, we wish it distinctly understood, far easier to attain than is generally supposed; and which, even to many of those long wrenched by bad habits or by illness, must not be despaired of, but perseveringly striven for, as, in reason, probable and almost certain yet to attain.

CHAPTER 1

EFFECTS OF A SOUND BODY

Among the signs of manly health and perfect physique, internal and external, are a clear eye, a transparent and perhaps embrowned complexion (this latter not necessarily), an upright attitude, a springy step, a sweet breath, a ringing voice and little or nothing of irritability in the temper. With your choleric man, there is apt to be something wrong in the stomach, joints or blood. In nine cases out of ten, when this is obviated the disposition comes round.

We shall speak by and by of health as being the foundation of all real manly beauty. Perhaps, too, it has more to do than is generally supposed, with the capacity of being agreeable as a companion, a social visitor, always welcome—and with the divine joys of friendship. In these particulars (and they surely include a good part of the best blessings of existence) there is that subtle virtue in a sound body, with all its functions perfect, which nothing else can make up for, and which will itself make up for many other deficiencies, as of education, refinement, and the like.

We have even sometimes fancied that there was a wonderful medicinal effect in the mere personal presence of a man who was perfectly well! While, on the other hand, what can be more debilitating than to be continually surrounded by sickly people, and to have to do with them only?

REASON — OUR OBJECTS

It is not too much to begin to demand of the young men, and indeed the masses of the people, (through conscientious writers for the press, speakers, etc.), that, in this great matter of health and a manly form and soundness, steady reason should assume the helm, and keep it.

We know that to many this will seem advice whose accomplishment, on anything like a general scale, is out of the question. Yet we confess we are hopeful of its success, in time. For where, we repeat, is there a man, young, old, or middle-aged, who does not mainly desire to have a perfect physique?

The object we have in view is the presentation in a collected and connected form, for popular use, of the general run of facts, rules, suggestions, etc., most desirable to be understood by those who have not yet paid any earnest attention to the subject of developing a perfect and manly physique. These, indeed, the common classes, and young men, form the immense body, the audience to whom our hints are, in the main, directed. It will, therefore, be necessary for us to go over some of the grounds that may be familiar to those of our readers who have already studied out the subject. Still it will do them also no harm to go over the same statements again. Indeed, it is probable that, of three-fourths of the young and middle-aged men, not only in this city of New York, but in every portion of the United States, one of the best goods they could do for themselves would be the careful reading, once or twice every year, during the remainder of their lives, of all these paragraphs we are now writing.

Our object is, at the same time, to be attained in our own rambling and discursive way, and our writing will be without technical terms and phrases; for we are free to confess ourselves as no physician— but one who, by observation and study, has come to view the theme of health as oftentimes able to be better treated, for popular use, by an outsider, than a medical man—for whoever knew one of the latter to write a treatise, except its main direction were to the medical fraternity more than any others?

We would have gymnasia commenced, so as gradually to form part of all the public schools of America, even from Maine to Texas, and from the northern boundary of Washington Territory to the southern point of Florida. This, no doubt, sounds extravagant to the superficial reader, but by him who has investigated the subject, and is aware how, under all circumstances, proper training trebles the natural power, endurance, and health of the body, it will be better understood. There is even no hunter, warrior, wild Indian, or the strongest and supplest backwoodsman of the West, but would have all his natural qualities increased far beyond what they are, by judicious training. This is art, the province of which is to take natural germs or gifts, and bring them out in the fullest and best way.

A FINE ANIMAL MAN

Do not be startled at the words, excellent reader. It is, in our view, indispensably necessary that a man should be a fine animal—sound and vigorous. This, to be candid with you, is the text and germ of most of our remarks—which arise out of it, and seek to promulgate and explain how it can be fully accomplished. It being the specialty of these articles makes it necessary to consider all that belongs to you, reader, and to your body, structure, etc., mostly from that point of view alone. And why should we not? Almost everything else is attended to but the animal part of a man—as if that were something to be ashamed of and repressed. Indeed, this is avowedly the theory of many very good people, who proceed upon it in the bringing up of their children.

That such is not our theory is of course evident, or will be, in every line of these articles. We, at the same time, know with the rest that a man has a moral, affectional, and mental nature which must also be developed; but we say that, at present, the whole tendency of things is to over-develop those parts, while the physical is cramped and dwindled away.

Yes, reader, we teach that man must be perfect in his body first— we start with that as our premises, our foundation. We would throw into something like regular form a few principal hints and suggestions. Now this is to be done. Would that other writers, and that teachers also, would follow up in the same train of influence with ourselves— until there should be no man, especially any young man, through the length and breadth of the land, who should any longer be allowed to plead ignorance of these simple laws as a reason for his impaired constitution and loss of man's physique.

Gratified indeed should we be if we thought these hints were the means of arresting the attention of this younger part of the American people, and recalling them to a sense of that, which, once having it, is not at all difficult to restrain, but once thoroughly lost, may be mourned and sought for long afterward in vain—and even when restored must be watched over with double the former care. But yet we will not discourage any of those who having injured their health, seek to regain it. We would rather impress upon them the probability, almost certainty, under prudent management, of attaining their sound condition again.

FOR STUDENTS, CLERKS, AND THOSE IN SEDENTARY OR MENTAL EMPLOYMENTS

Can there then be no such thing as hard study going on without detriment to health—for study is mental exercise? We have elsewhere hinted that there not only can, but that study may go on favourably to health. Only all study, and no developed physique, is death. Our readers must take a broad and deep view of our arguments, from our own points of observation; for we have not time to fill up the gaps, and connect one item with another as we would, if we had nothing else to do. At present, a few suggestive points must answer, and we are confident we are talking to people of intelligent minds and who know something of this subject already.

We say to the young man not only that mental development may well go on at the same time with physical development, but that indeed is the only way in which they should go on—both together, which is much to the advantage of each. If you are a student, be also a student of the body, a practitioner of manly exercises, realizing that a broad chest, a muscular pair of arms, and two sinewy legs, will be just as much credit to you, and stand you in hand through your future life, equally with your geometry, your history, your classics, your law, medicine, or divinity. Let nothing divert you from your duty to your body. Up in the morning early! Habituate yourself to the brisk walk in the fresh air—to the exercise of pulling the oar—and to the loud declamation upon the hills, or along the shore. Such are the means by which you can seize with treble gripe upon all the puzzles and difficulties of your student life—whatever problems are presented to you in your books, or by your professors. Guard your manly power, your health and strength, from all hurts and violations—this is the most sacred charge you will ever have in your keeping.

8

To you, clerk, literary man, sedentary person, man of fortune, idler, the same advice. Up! The world (perhaps you now look upon it with pallid and disgusted eyes) is full of zest and beauty for you, if you approach it in the right spirit! Out in the morning! If in the city, even there you will find ample sources of amusement and interest in its myriad varieties of character and occupation—in the scenes of its awakening and adjusting itself to its daily labors—in the crowds around its ferries, and all through its main thoroughfares, and at its great depots and markets. Do not be discouraged soon. Give our advice a thorough trial—not for a few days or weeks, but for months. Early rising, early to bed, exercise, plain food, thorough and persevering continuance in gently-commenced training, the cultivation with resolute will of a cheerful temper, the society of friends and a certain number of hours spent every day in regular employment—these, we say, simple as they are, are enough to revolutionize life, and change it from a scene of gloom, feebleness, and irresolution, into life indeed, as becomes such a universe as this, full of all the essential means of happiness, full of well-intentioned and affectionate men and women, with the beneficent processes of nature always at work, the sun shining, the flowers blooming, the crops growing, the waters running, with all else that is wanted, only that man should be rightly toned to partake of the universal strength and joy. This he must do through reason, knowledge and exercise—in short, through training; for that is the sum of all.

CHAPTER 2

TO MORALISTS, REFORMERS, ETC.

IT IS OUR deeply felt conviction, the result of much observation in New York, Brooklyn, and other cities, that the only true and profitable way of reaching the morals of the young is through making them first, healthy, clean-blooded, and vigorous specimens of men. The wisest preacher, teacher, or philanthropist is not he who is forever dwelling on abstract qualities, off in the clouds, or that would make virtuous bloodless phantoms of our young men. That can never be; and yet we believe that, out of health and a fine physique, would arise an immensely greater development of morality and abstract good.

At present there is mutual recoil between the pure moralist and the teacher of healthy bodily exercises and games—which recoil, in our opinion, should not exist at all. It was not so formerly. The young men of Athens, and other Greek cities, were trained in their bodily, mental, and moral developments and perfections together, and this, as we have before intimated, is the only way, indeed, in which training can be just to the whole man. We repeat, however, that the first requisite to a young man is that he should be well and hardy; and that from such a foundation alone, he will be more apt to become good, upright, friendly, and self-respected.

LIFE WITHOUT A SOUND BODY WHAT IS IT GOOD FOR?

Reason seems to tell a man, not so much that death is dreadful, as that dragging out a useless, deficient, and sickly life is dreadful. We even think that if such a life were to be continued year after year, without probability of change, death would be preferable—would be a happy relief from it.

This being so, the great object of a man's exertions should be, commencing before he is a man, even in early youth, to lay the foundations of a sound and capable life, by forming for himself a sound and capable body. It is all in vain to say, (though practically our civilized life does say so, in many forms) that a sick, unsound, or prematurely dying man, has a life really worth living for. And when we come to consider what vast swarms of these sick men, (or at least not-well men) there are, the fact is one which looms up in terrible proportions!

Yes, we repeat it, there is more distress and horror in one unhappy life, made so by the want of stamina and tone, than in the mere fact of a hundred deaths. Let, then, the attention be given to making life worth the possession; let manly health and physique be oftener taught, and strenuously attended to.

ATHLETICISM

One of the objects we have in view in presenting these statements to the reader is to help on the taste for athletic exercises and wholesome games, which seems to be sprouting up in New York, Brooklyn, and other American cities. This subject of athleticism (we will coin a new word, and what seems to us a needed one) cannot be mentioned with-out the thoughts irresistibly turning back to ancient Greece, where it received its fullest attention, and, in return, aided with other means in making them the most physically and intellectually glorious nation of antiquity.

The Grecian manly games (we may mention, for the interest in them is ever fresh) consisted of five principle exercises, running races on foot, leaping, boxing, wrestling, and throwing the discus or quoit— all of which we inherit from that ancient time and people.

Running was the exercise held in the highest estimation—and the name of the victor in it, was often identified with the Olympiad in which he had gained the triumph. It was probably prepared for by far more careful antecedents than with us; the contestants were very numerous, and the prize, an olive crown, was considered the most honorable token it lay in the power of man to attain. It is to be mentioned that the pre-examination of those who contended in these games was very strict, and that a temperate, chaste, moral, and heroic life, for a long period previously, was indispensable. (How many of our modern young men, under these tests, would have a chance of competing?)

The boxing games were dangerous and bloody, and often resulted in death. The combatants covered their fists with the cestus, which had an effect something like the "iron knuckles" of our modern sporting men, being a glove made of straps of leather, plated inside with metal. The boxers were the fiercest and roughest of the ancient athletes. They were always noticed to be more or less maimed, some with the loss of an eye, or of the teeth, or a broken nose, or frightful gashes in the face.

Leaping was performed as with us. Wrestling required great address and experience, and was a great physical art. In the arena, several matches would be going on at the same time. The wrestlers were naked, and had their bodies anointed with oil.

There was a contest, called the Pancratium, with included all means of defense and offense, at the option of the fighter, who was expected to do the best he could for himself, and the worst for his adversary. It was lawful to scratch, bite, gouge, kick—in short, just like a modern Arkansas rough-and-tumble of the severest kind, barring the bowie knife.

These games, in which all were interested and most of the young and middle-aged men partook, served to make a very hardy and handsome-bodied race. In such severe exercises, the Greeks not only prepared themselves for the hardships and contests of war, but for the enjoyment of life, and to acquire a happy and vigorous national temper. Nor were they, for all these rough exercises, a brutal or bloody-minded race; but, on the contrary, were friendly, tender-hearted, affectionate and benevolent.

But the manly exercises we are describing did not comprehend the physique only. In the Olympic and other great games, there were intellectual contests also. The poets, orators and historians took part, contended for prizes, and recited their productions before the people. There were also songs, dances, and musical instruments.

Here, too, on such occasions, the sculptors, painters and artists exhibited specimens of their skill—while the philosophers and teachers moved around, or drew groups together, to hear their arguments and disputes.

We will only add to our brief description that these great games always commenced at daybreak, and were mainly held during the forenoon—different from our modern plan of presenting amusements at night. They were also invariably held in the open air.

From them, we repeat, the Greeks become one of the healthiest, handsomest, hardiest, and happiest nations that ever lived.

MENTALITY, STUDY, ETC., IN THEIR RELATIONS TO HEALTH

We should like to say much on the various phases of this interesting topic. A high degree of mental development is generally supposed to be analogous to a delicate state of health. So strongly is this style of judgment fixed in the popular mind, that a person of robust physique can seldom or never obtain the credit of having a cultivated mind and a great brain. There is just this amount of truth in the popular ideas on this subject, that a man of refined mentality, and of good knowledge of physiology, will be far more liable to be injured by pernicious and unsanitary habits, than persons of low grade who have the same average strength of constitution and vigor with himself.

Any one may notice this, as it is illustrated in the low-life shanties, and in all places, both city and country, where the lowest order of the population reside. In utter defiance of all the laws of physiology, we see it arise, from the denizens of those places, some of the most splendid specimens of health and physical beauty in the world. Indeed, take the case through, it is doubtful whether the upper ranks of society, with all their superior advantages, produce as many specimens of well-built and fine-appearing men, clean-blooded and sound, as these very places where health is never thought of, and, in appearance, is constantly violated.

This fact, which is so startling at first, and seems to knock spots out of all our calculations and advice, will, when further investigated, be found to come under the simple and true theory of health, and confirm it just the same as the rest. The children of a poor family, especially in the country, and to a great extent in cities also, are never injured by those pampering luxuries and

13

condiments that are frequently the bane of the offspring of the rich—who are often literally killed by kindness. The former, if weak and puny, are perhaps more apt to die off, leaving only the hardier shoots to buffet the storms and exposures of life. And these hardier shoots are often found to thrive all the better from such exposures and trials. Like plants left to grow where they first sprouted out of the ground, intended by the gardener, left to the nursing of the sunshine, the air, and the rains, they thrive and attain a wild and hardy beauty which the most carefully tended of their more artificial brethren seek in vain to rival. This, however, is the result of a happy combination of circumstances, all of which, as we have just said, conform to the general laws of health.

For he who is determined to reach, and experience for a continued time, the condition of perfect health, will do well to understand that caution is necessary, lest he overdo the matter. There is such a thing as taking too minute and morbid care of the health, and, therefore, losing it as effectually as by taking no care at all. This is a remark which will apply to those who are on the rack every hour lest something may not be exactly right with themselves or their children; and especially to those who over-protect themselves against cold, the air, and exposure.

Let it be known that a certain degree of abandon is necessary to the processes of perfect health and a muscular tone of the system. The fault of intellectual persons is, doubtless, not only that far too much of their general, natural fund of stimulation is diverted, year after year, from all the great organs in the trunk of the body, and concentrated in the brain, but that they think too much of health, and, perhaps, that they know too much of its laws. Of this last, it might be explained that if they only knew a little more, namely, to put their technical knowledge aside at times, and not be forever dwelling upon it, things would go on much better with them.

With all this, we have an idea, amounting to profound conviction that the highest and palmiest state of health, ministering to a long life, and accompanied throughout by all that makes a man physically the superior animal of the earth, and crowned at last with a painless and easy death—we have an idea, we say, that all this is only attainable, (except in rare natural instances) by a cultivated mentality, by the intellectual, by the reasoning man.

14

What else, indeed, is the whole system of training for physique, but intellect applied to the bettering of the form, the blood, the strength, the life, of man?

In other and shorter terms, true intellectual development, not over-strained and morbid, is highly favorable to long life, and a noble physique; and what falls short of these latter aims, (if attributable to anything in the mentality of the subject) is, that the mentality of that subject was in a vitiated condition, or, (as in these latter days is often the case) that there was not enough brute animal in the man. We repeat it, strange as it may seem this is generally the case in these extra-mental and extra-philanthropic days of ours.

That the half-way and unwholesomely developed mentality of modern times, as seen in large classes of people, literary persons, many in the professions, in sedentary employments, etc., acts injuriously upon the health, and militates against the noble form, the springy gait, the ruddy cheek and lip, and the muscular leg and arm of man, we know, full well. But, without wishing to be severe, what, critically considered, is the amount of modern mentality, except a feverish, superficial and shallow dealing with words and shams? How many of these swarms of "intellectual people," so-called, are anything but smatterers, needing yet to begin and educate themselves in nearly all real knowledge and wisdom?

TRAINING

There we print the magic word that can remedy all the troubles and accomplish all the wonders of human physique. Training! In its full sense, it involves the entire science of manly excellence, education, beauty, and vigor—nor is it without intimate bearings upon the moral and intellectual nature.

Human reason applied to develop the perfection of the body and the mind! What can there be more worthy? We are not insensible to the triumphs of the demonstrative sciences and philosophy—to the explanation of the subtleties of mind—to the accomplishment of such wonders as the Atlantic Telegraph, the great feat of the age; but for all that, we are clear in the opinion of

15

the still greater importance of all these researches and statements directly affecting individual happiness and health—the development of a superb race of men, large-bodied, clean-blooded, and with all the attributes of the best material humanity. We believe this is one of the most commendable departments in which the philanthropist can exercise his time and abilities—and that literature, and the public essayist and lecturer, would do well to pay it more attention, and include it more frequently in their themes.

Development! Few understand, (you, reader, probably as little as any one) what a fund of physical power is in them, which systematic training could bring forth, and increase to marvelous proportions.

Look at the brawny muscles attached to the arms of that young man, who, for nearly two years past, has devoted on an average two hours out of the twenty-four to rowing in a boat, swinging the dumb-bells, or exercising with the Indian club. Look at the spread of his manly chest, on which also are flakes of muscle which rival those of the ox or horse.—(Start not, delicate reader! the comparison is one to be envied.)

Two years ago that same young man was puny, hollow-breasted, walking home at evening with a languid gait, and eating his meals with less than half an appetite. Training, and the simplest amount of perseverance, has altogether made a new being of him.

Training, however, it is always to be borne in mind, does not consist in mere exercise. Equally important with that are the diet, drink, habits, sleep, etc. Bathing, the breathing of good air, and certain other requisites, are also not to be overlooked. But of the details of these, we shall speak directly.

To Vocalists and public speakers, lawyers, lecturers, actors, etc., training is always to be recommended. We not only allude to habitual practising with the voice, but to great care in diet and drink. Of course, it is well understood among vocalists, that long and steady practice is the only ladder by which they can mount to success. But among the other classes we have mentioned, there is hardly ever any fit preparation for entering on their profession, as regards its physical requirements. We see, indeed, a majority of public speakers, with narrow chests, feeble lungs, diseased throats, and poor voices.

Gentle and gradual development of the vocal powers is within the reach of all; and so, by degrees, to the acquisition of a very remarkable scope of the voice. In oratory, in all ages, they who have attained the highest and most lasting fame have been those who, by slow and patient processes, have trained themselves, their voices, their movements, etc. This is art, which is as necessary for any great thing as the natural genius for it. Art cannot, of course, give original life, but it can shape and form it to great things, and to beautiful proportions.

Of all who have to speak, sing, or converse much, etc., the diet is important. The simplest and most natural diet is the best; and lest we be misunderstood, we specify that we do not mean a vegetarian or water-gruel diet, but one of strengthening materials, beef, lamb, etc., and that fruits, wines, and the like, are not to be excluded. But indulgence in a great variety of dishes at the same meal, and, in general terms, the absorption into the system of fat, or any indigestible substance, or the drinking of strong coffee or liquors, will be pretty sure to injure the voice.

Here, as in many things, we gain serviceable hints from the ancients, and their way in similar circumstances. Of the actors in the theatre of Bacchus, in Athens, where the tragedies of Sophocles and the other Greek poets were played, it is recorded that they observed a rigid diet, in order to give strength and clearness to their vocalization, and that they regularly frequented gymnasiums, in order to acquire muscular energy and pliancy of limbs.

We commend all this to our young American students for the bar, the pulpit, or any other avocation requiring oratorical power; and also to not a few of the actors and singers.

CHAPTER 3

BRIEF SKETCH OF A DAY OF TRAINING, FOR THE USE OF BEGINNERS

A FINE LESSON may be learned from the observance and history of the operation of putting a man in perfect condition for any great feat of strength and agility, such as a prize fight, a foot race, running, or the like. The trainers will sometimes take such a man, every way in a bad state, physically, from injurious habits of eating and drinking, want of exercise, etc., his blood bad, his complexion spotted with pimples, his joints nerveless, his tone and vigor at a very low ebb, his digestion poor, his pulse flighty, his animal temperature subject to great inward changes of heat and cold—and will, after gradually inaugurating them, establish such changes in his habits as will turn that man out in a few weeks a completely renovated being, feeling well, looking well, with his muscular development carried to its ultimate degree of perfection, and all the bad humours drenched from his body.

Inquire how this wonderful change is wrought, and you will learn that it, by only a few and the most simple means, all of which lie in the reach of every man, and are not, after all, so very unpleasant in themselves, can be carried on consistently with the usual trade or employment of a mechanic, farmer, or any workingman.

In many cases, (though we do not think this quite so necessary as has been supposed—or rather, we believe the results can be attained just as well by other means) it is usual to begin the operation of training a man by clearing out the system with medicine, an ordinary cathartic, (salts, or whatever else is found to answer the purpose) and an emetic. This puts the stomach and bowels in a fit state for the future work.

From the first, of course, the greatest care is observed in the food. At the time of taking the clearing out medicine, only a little light aliment is given; and when the medicinal effects are worked off, which will be in a day or two, the man in training, if he be of too full habit, too heavy, must be restricted to a moderate diet, including, for a while, only one substantial meal of meat a-day; the breakfast being limited to a small portion of meat, or perhaps a nearly raw egg, a slice of dry bread, and, if desired, a cup of tea, to be drank only when quite cool.

The man rises at day-break or soon after— if in winter, rather before. In most cases the best thing he can commence the day with is a rapid wash of the whole body in cold water, using a sponge, or the hands rubbing the water over the body—and then coarse towels to rub dry with; after which, the hair gloves, the flesh-brush, or anything handy, may be used, for friction, and to put the skin in a red glow all over. This, especially in cool weather, must all be done in a few minutes, or rather moments—not much longer than you have taken to read about it. Meanwhile, as soon as the glow is attained, the window, unless the weather is very bad, should be opened, and the door also, so that the room may become filled with good fresh air— for the play of the respiratory organs will be increased by the performances just mentioned, and it is at such times that good air tells best. Keep briskly moving all this while, however.

There is no objection, when this is through, to the man taking a crust of bread, or a piece of sea-biscuit. Then for a brisk walk, or some other exercise, of half an hour, or an hour, according to circumstances; at this, very heavy soled shoes, carrying weight, may be used— lighter at first and increased by degrees. Or if one is not inclined for a walk, the dumb-bells, or some gymnastic exercises. Whatever is done, however, ought to be in the open air; don't be afraid of that—drink it in—it won't hurt you—there is a curious virtue in it, to be found in nothing else.

This brings us to an early breakfast hour. Usually the breakfast, for a hearty man, might consist in a plate of fresh rare lean meat, without fat or gravy, a slice or chunk of bread, and, if desired, a cup of tea, which must be left till the last. If there be boiled potatoes, and one of them is desired, it may be permitted. Ham, gravy, fried potatoes, and a list too long and numerous to mention, of dishes often found on the breakfast table of boarding houses and restaurants, must be eschewed. Fortunately, there is hardly a table set but it affords something that will answer, at a pinch, for a meal.

The great art lies in what to avoid and what to deny one's self.

After breakfast, in the case of a man who has work to do, (for we are writing for the general public, as well as the sporting man) he will go about his employment. One who has not, and who is devoting his attention, at the time, to the establishment of health and a manly physique, will do well to spend an hour of the forenoon (say from 10 to 11 o'clock) in some good exercises for the arms, hands, breast, spine, shoulders, and waist; the dumb-bells, sparring, or a vigorous attack on the sand-bags, (a large bag, filled with sand, and suspended in such a position that it can be conveniently struck with the fists.) This should be done systematically, and gradually increased upon making the exertion harder and harder.

A pretty long walk may also be taken, commencing at an ordinary pace, and increasing the rapidity of the step till it takes the power of locomotion pretty well, and then keeping it up at that gait, as it can be well endured—not to the extent of fatigue, however, for it is a law of training that a man must not exercise so hard at any time as to overdo and tire himself; but always stop in time to avoid fatigue. We mean, of course, the sense of being fagged out, wearied, unable to do any more. We repeat the caution elsewhere given, to take everything very moderately and gently at first, and let all come on by slow degrees.

Rowing is also a good exercise during this time of day. Those engaged in this as their regular employment, (we may say, en passant) ought to understand that they have one of the finest occupations in the world, for health, strength, and a fine development of form. By a tolerable attention to the laws of physiology, they could present a race of men, almost without exception for vigor, and for manly beauty.

From three quarters to half an hour before dinner, all violent exercise must cease. If the body is sweaty, as it very likely will be, it is best to strip, rub down briskly with dry cloths, and change the underclothes.

Dinner should consist of a good plate of fresh meat, (rare lean beef, broiled or roast, is best) with as few outside condiments as possible. (If thirsty during the forenoon, drink, but never before eating.) Eat according to your appetite, of one dish—always, if possible, making four or five dinners out of the week, of rare lean beef, with nothing else than a small slice of stale bread. Or, if preferred, lean mutton, cooked rare, may be eaten instead of beef, at times, for variety. No scraggly, grisly fat, or hard cooked pieces, should be eaten. Nor need the appetite be stinted—eat enough, and when you eat that, stop!

No man should be required to do any toilsome work or exercise immediately after dinner; if there be anything you know you will have to take hold of immediately, then make the dinner lighter, for it is more hurtful than is supposed, to exert one's physical powers greatly, on a hearty meal.

(We cannot resist the impulse to condemn here, what we consider the frightfully injurious dinners and dinner habits of most people who, as they would call it, "live well." Look over the bill of fare of any hotel or restaurant, or even the dinner-table of an ordinary boarding-house—see the incongruous dishes that, on the bills, stand in long lists, and that men devour, often three or four different kinds—soups, pastry, fat, fish, flesh, gravy, pickles, pie, pudding, coffee, water, ale, brandy—and heaven knows what else! Not one out of fifty eats a really wholesome, manly substantial dinner. All, more or less, distend the stomach, and bloat themselves with quantities of trash, to worry the digestion, thin the blood, and return, sooner or later, in lassitude, headache, constipation, or a fever, or some other attack of illness.)

The afternoon, unless it be spent in the regular work—and in most cases, unless it be a prize fight or the like, we believe that the operation of training a man for his condition may go on just as well, if he continue about his daily work. The afternoon may be spent with the same objects in view as the morning. If, during the latter, the exercises have tended to develop the chest and arms, the afternoon may be devoted more to the locomotive organs. A long walk may be taken—or a good game at leaping, or any of the games that tax the legs—straddling, standing on one leg and dipping to the ground, so as to touch the other knee, etc.

We have thus indicated the mode of filling up the hours of the day; but still more is necessary. After a moderate supper, of some digestible dish, fruit, or cold meat, or stale bread, toast, or biscuit, with perhaps a cup of tea—the evenings ought to be devoted, to some extent at least, to friendly and social recreation, (not dissipation, remember.) Friends may be visited, or some amusement, or a stroll in company—or any other means that will soothe and gratify the mind and the affections, friendship, etc.—for every man should pride himself on having such affections, and satisfying them, too.

Ten o'clock at night ought to find a man in bed—for that will not afford him the time requisite for rest, if he rise betimes in the morning. The bedroom must not be small and close—that would go far toward spoiling all other observances and cares for health. It is important that the system should be clarified, through the inspiration and respiration, with a plentiful supply of good air, during the six, seven, or eight hours that are spent in sleep. During most of the year, the window must be kept partly open for this purpose.

WHO CAN FOLLOW RULES?

Such is the exclamation we fancy we hear from the reader, upon perusing what appear to him, no doubt, at first, very hard requirements. What man, among the masses who, in their various occupations, toil for their living, in city or country, can possibly conform to the strict letter of these laws of health? Have not most people enough to do to get something to eat, without being so very particular what it shall be, and how it is cooked?

We are well aware that, to those unaccustomed to consider the laws of health and a sound physique, there will appear at first some- thing quite alarming and impracticable in these requirements. But they are really more so in appearance, and from their novelty, than anything else. So long as a man has to have something purchased for his sustenance, why may he not as well have that which is best, as that which is no good? On the score of economy, we have everything on our side—and, under what we promulgate; the expenses of living would be reduced at least one third.

We know, at the same time, that men in various employments have not that chance of following out their judgment and choice in these things that would allow of their rigidly fulfilling the laws, at every point. Yet even these can come a great deal nearer the fulfillment than they now suppose. It needs mainly the knowledge and determination in a man's self—then all becomes comparatively easy, and obstacles melt away, one after another.

Besides, we are willing to admit that our exact statements with regard to diet—what must be avoided, and the few simple articles of food that, coincident with exercise, strength, digestion, etc., may be used—are to be often modified to suit cases, tastes, etc., each one for itself. We have made the statement of a model case; if the reader approaches the neighborhood of it, he will be doing well.

MORAL RESULTS OF TRAINING

The results of properly chosen and well-continued courses of training are so valuable and so numerous that in mentioning them we would seem to be mentioning most of the precious treasures of character—among the rest may be specified courage, quickness of all the perceptions, full use of power, independence, fortitude, good nature, a hopeful and sunny temper, an industrious disposition, temperance in all the alimentative appetites, chastity, an aversion to artificial indulgences, easy manners without affectation, personal magnetism, and a certain silent eloquence of expression, and a general tendency to the wholesome virtues and to that moral uprightness which arises out of and is the counterpart to the physical.

For we cannot too often and too strongly promulgate the fact of the inevitable and curious conjunction, or rather resultance, of a fine manly moral character, out of a perfect physique. If there be those of our sporting fraternities who fail in realizing this point, it is so much loss to them and to their completeness of development, even on their own terms and for their own purposes. Why should it be so? There is truly no reason for it. The true theory and the indications are all the other way.

We are of those who believe, therefore, that a certain natural moral goodness is developed in proportion with a sound physical development—and also that a true system of training, that which aims to do justice to the complete man and his highest powers, (and what other system deserves the name?) will on no account, ignore the seeds and fruits of a noble moral character.

This much we feel impelled to say, because confident are we

not only that those called under the general name of the sporting fraternity, and, indeed, all who take an interest, or have a part in, physical training and manly games and exercises, would be vastly improved in their own special branches, by realizing this moral part of the theory of training, which, indeed, is its crowning glory and natural result—but we are equally sure that there exists, through all the grades and classes we have just alluded to, the very stuff and material of the kind of superior qualities we demand. They may be, doubtless are, in the crude and rough state—but they are there.

Reader, if you be one of that exclusive kind who suppose that manly actions and an honorable character belong only to one or two departments of society, and those the ones that profess the greatest virtue, let us undeceive you—let us hint to you that perhaps there is equal, possibly at times even greater manliness and heroism, in what are called less pious degrees of the social strata—even that very sporting fraternity we spoke of.

WE DO NOT INCULCATE A MERE PASTIME

Of exercises, games, gymnastics, etc., the reader must understand well that we inculcate the regular and appropriate practising of them not as a frivolous pastime, or a matter of ceremony and politeness, to be done in a genteel club way, but as a real live thing, a part of a robust and perfect man. And all the rest of the habits are to be consistent. There is no sham or make-believe about this business of entering on the development, purification, strengthening and gracefulness of the body; but it is something to be carried out with an earnest, conscientious, persevering soul.

We say conscientiously, and we mean all that is involved in the word. The man must himself feel the importance of the objects to be attained, and an enthusiastic, yet in a certain sense calm determination to strive for them, not for a little while merely, but for a long while, at work or play, in company or alone, in one place or another, and night and day. Habit will soon make all easy; and let us inform you, reader, there is no small pleasure in the victory one attains, by a little sternness of will, over all deleterious gratifications of appetite. It is as great as a general

24

gaining an important battle.

BACKSLIDING FROM HEALTHY HABITS

Let us be plain with you, reader. Under the impulse of studying our articles, and awakened very strongly to the idea of health and a strong condition, you will very likely commence carrying into practice the advice we have jotted down for your benefit. After a shorter or longer time, it is quite certain to us there will be a relapse, however, into the old and more careless ways. A great revolution, a new system of physical habits, cannot be inaugurated quite so easily as you thought. Consequently, with the best intentions in the world, there is still lamentable backsliding.

But the work must not be given up for the first failure—or even for the second, third, nor any number. It will gradually grow easier and easier, and habit will then make it followed, without thinking anything about it.

It is a great pity that about half the time spent by preachers and teachers in attention to moral and intellectual training, were not dispensed with, and bestowed on the encouragement of young men in training and perfecting their bodies. As things are, the subject is seldom mentioned in a way to arouse the lethargic, urge on the flagging, and reward those who have set a noble example.

It must be realized, throughout, that perpetual care is indispensable to health. It is just as reasonable to suppose you can squander your fortune at random, and still find it remaining at the end of many years, as that you can squander your health and have that remain. Look at those young mechanics, in Boston, New York, or Philadelphia! Look at the many fine specimens of drivers, teamsters, firemen, lumbermen, hay-men, pilots, etc.! What examples of strength, beauty, and activity! What fine color in the complexion—grace in the movement—heartiness in the whole structure and appearance! Is it not lamentable that, for the want of a little knowledge and care, all these noble blessings will, probably, by degrees, be lost to them, far too prematurely? For, let us inform you, reader, if you be young, that the years of your middle age ought to be those not only of your best performances, but of your best appearance—and, if you so will it, may be. Then all has become ripe and mature; and surely the fully ripened fruit or flower is no less beautiful and welcome than any stage which precedes it.

Such are the reflections which must often arise from an observant person, at seeing the way in which American young men scatter the rich treasures of their health, to grow old before their time, and to lose, perhaps, the best and mellowest portion of life, a happy middle, and a contented old age.

TRAINING ALL THROUGH LIFE

This carries us to another statement. He who has the idea of proficiency in any art, as music for example, will understand of what importance it is to keep in perpetual practice. Well, it is of just as much, or rather, it is of infinitely more importance that he who would be a proficient in manly health and strength, should also keep in perpetual practice.

As things are, it is only on some extra occasion, as a race, a physical contest in the prize ring, etc., that men submit themselves to training. But we would have it a regular and systematic thing through life. Not only in young manhood, but in middle age, and in advanced age, also, modified to suit its appropriate requirements, should the course of training be persevered in, without intermission. We place the greatest reliance upon the forming of the habit, and therefore repeat it many times in these articles.

Neither season, place, nor circumstance should prevent the regular course of training, or as near to it as matters will allow. It is the resolution, the disposition, that is of the main consequence; with that, all obstacles will be overcome. The true benefits of training, indeed, lie in their permanent continuance; it is an affair for the whole life.

We would have exercises for all ages, without excepting any—requiring only that they should be fitted properly to each stage, modified to each individual case. There is no time of life to which the training processes do not apply, and would not improve those who use them, both for the time being and subsequently. As to the objection to any gymnastic exercises, that they are only fitted for young and robust men, and not for the feeble or old, we reply that the true and comprehensive system of gymnastics must include exercises appropriate to those very cases of weak, or very young, or more advanced persons, or else it is no complete system, and needs to be improved upon.

Yes, training for all ages of life, each adjusted to peculiarities, wants, and circumstances—always tenderly considering the average ability of the person, young or old, to bear fatigue, and never overtaxing or straining his powers, but letting them gradually and gently develop themselves.

One of the faults to be guarded against, in gymnastic, and indeed all the exercises of training, is the wish to get along too fast. The body is too complicated and exquisite a piece of work to be suddenly brought to bear upon, for any lasting good effects of this sort. It ought to be considered enough if the general course of exercise, health and development be started in the right direction, and kept in it, and then let the results be patiently waited for.

OVERTASKING

We must dwell a moment especially here. Let it not be supposed that this question of exercise presents but one side, and that evil to the general health comes from not enough activity. Much is to be said also of the injury of casually overtasking the frame, as is done by many persons, and often at the very times of life when the injury is most fatal to the future soundness and perfection of the body—we mean youth and early manhood. This we think markedly the case in the country, among the farmers. The boys are put to hard work there too soon, and kept at it too tight. That is the reason we see (for such is the truth) fewer manly and agile forms among the young men of the country than those of the city.

Excessive toil, whether of the body or the mind, is just as hurtful to health and longevity, be it understood, as the stagnant condition of the organs which it has been the drift of our preceding remarks to guard against. We would also caution the young men against any very violent draughts upon the strength, such as an exhausting struggle or run, when the body is not prepared for it by previous training. It may have to be paid for very dearly.

Carpenters, masons, farmers, laborers, men at work on the shipping, and all at active outdoor occupations; of course have a

27

fair share of exercise already. This is so much gained. With them, however, it by no means follows but that a steady and judicious course of athletic training, from time to time, (whenever not prevented by the occasionally severe toll which makes rest the thing wanted) would greatly improve their physical capacities also. Those parts of the body should be especially attended to which are least called into use by the trade or occupation; for instance, drivers should develop the use and strength of the legs, by walking, leaping, pushing weights with the feet, etc.

Clerks, bookkeepers, literary persons, etc., need a regular, but never too violent, exercise of the whole of the frame, chest, arms, spine, legs and feet. They need early rising, simple food, and, almost always, would be bettered by acquiring more of an animal physique—unfashionable though it be.

Merchants, lawyers, professional people, politicians, etc., (and perhaps the American people generally) need a little more contentment of mind—the disposition to enjoy life and not fret, but to be happy with moderation or even a little.

STANDARD OF HEALTH

Take notice, as we talk, that our standard of health is not a small one, but a high one. Many of those who dash about, city and country, with an artificial glow, kept up by the excitement of company or business, and ready to collapse the moment those impulses are withdrawn, such are by no means our models of health. We speak of the real article, able to stand a great deal of buffeting and deprivation—health deeply founded, ingrained with the life, calculated to last many years, and (being encouraged by regular habits) more to be noticed by its quiet, steady, and continued movement, than by any abrupt and striking manifestations.

It is no small thing to be perfectly well. The case is one, in our civilized and artificial forms of life, alas, how rare! It is useless to blink the unpleasant conviction that in America, all through the large cities, and even in the country, where it might be less expected, the amount of ill-health, or just passable health, is enormous! Consumption, dyspepsia, rheumatism, chills and fever, and bilious attacks of one sort or another are met with in all directions.

Through the streets of New York, looking at the faces of a large majority of the men you pass—even the youths. They are not the faces of perfect health—and yet nearly all could be.

PRESENT CONDITION OF THE HEALTH OF THE MASSES

For it is not to be denied that physical inferiority, in one form or another, is the rule rather than the exception. Seriously examined, what a condition does the health of the masses everywhere present. Probably one-fourth of the whole population of the world dies of consumption, or of diseases that have sprouted up from it. Thousands upon thousands suffer from some form of scrofula, and are afflicted with sores and ulcers, interior or exterior. Half the people you meet have, at times, pimples and pustules on the face and neck, indicating that health is anything but clear with them. Indeed there are few, in any rank of life, but labor under some disorder of the blood.

Of late years, in the United States, the general illness, perhaps transcending all the rest, is dyspepsia. This is the fruitful mother of dozens of other complaints—for the regular and complete assimilation, digestion, and excretion, are the primal requisites of health. The fast living of Americans, and the general use of hot bread, grease, and strong coffee, are supposed to be the causes of this great New World complaint. But there are habits prevailing and articles of diet commonly eaten and imbibed as drink, in Germany, Holland, England, etc., far more indigestible than those just named, and yet the Dutch and English are not dyspeptic. What are the causes here?

Rheumatism is another prevalent complaint. Rare indeed, is the case of man or woman who has never felt a twinge of this distressing malady. Bilious attacks are very common in the west, and indeed in all parts of the land.

A too feverish life, mentally and physically, with too little physical calmness, and also a feeble paternity and maternity, are some of the main underlying causes of this frightful state of things. We are not disposed to grumble or overstate the evil condition of the public physique; we wish to call attention to the fact how easily most of these deficiencies might be remedied. Our theory is that America has mentality enough, but needs a far nobler physique.

THE GREAT AMERICAN EVIL—INDIGESTION

There can be no good health, or manly and muscular vigor to the system, without thorough and regular digestion. It is doubtless here that four-fifths of the weaknesses, breakings-down, and premature deaths, of American begin. On all sides we see the proofs of this last assertion—on all sides we see results of the same. If the harm that accrues to the physical perfection of the race, here in the United States, from this one cause, were obviated for the space of time long enough to allow a single generation to grow up and advance toward maturity, we should probably see the most splendid and majestic nation of men, in their physique, that ever trod the earth!

So great a part as that, does the little matter of the right digestion of the food we eat, bear upon the most momentous of sub-jects—for what can be more momentous than the growth of a per-fect race of men? All other rules and requisites may be attended to, but if the stomach be out of order, and allowed to remain so for any length of time, all will be of no avail. We are fain to alter one of the stereotyped sayings of the politicians, and say, Eternal vigilance is the price of— digestion!

In what is written so copiously on the subject of indigestion, it is customary to mention long lists of articles to be prohibited, and others

to be allowed. This is perhaps well enough—except that the reader will be led very far astray if he take it for granted that the whole story is told with that. It must also be understood that indigestion, and all its brood of evils, will take birth and grow to full proportions, from other causes, just as well as from the use of articles on the list of prohibited food. Indeed, if other things make up for it sufficiently, almost any article of food may be eaten with impunity. And if certain of these prime requisites of a good condition be wanting, why all the care in selecting aliment of easy digestion will be of no avail. How healthy, for instance, are the sailors, on their diet of salt beef, sea-biscuit, and strong coffee.

We do not intend here, great as the importance of this section of our subject is, to dwell minutely or at large upon it—partly because we think that each individual requires the application of special rules to his own particular case—partly because the subject of digestion is, in effect, treated and affected by the whole tenor of our paragraphs, under almost every one of the different headings of our subject—and partly because the main thing is to impress upon him who really wishes to acquire perfect health, that equal and thorough digestion is indispensable; and when that impression is produced, then the most a hasty writer on the subject can do, is done. Too many rules are apt to confuse—and besides they are liable to continual exceptions.

We say to you, reader, do justice to the peculiarities of your own case, with regard to your particular wants, strength, age, trade, previous and present circumstances, etc.; always having in view the main object, regular digestion. Do not depend on medicines to place your stomach in order; that is but casting out devils through Beelzebub, the prince of devils.

As a general thing, at a meal, if nothing very bad indeed is eaten, and if the selection of food be confined to dishes that relate to each other, and if the stomach be not deluged with liquid, it may do to follow, in reason, the demands of the taste and appetite. A few plain dishes, however, should always have the preference.

But it is perhaps apart from the body of our meals that indigestion takes its rise. We have been laying too much stress where it does not belong—like the man who denied himself a mild little glass of wine, and then ate a large dish of lobster salad, plastered over with oil and spices! If one were to be satisfied with eating his natural meals, following a natural appetite, and then stop, most of the trouble that exists would probably be avoided.

It is the after claps that do the mischief. Modern taste and ingenuity have contrived not a hundred, but hundreds of solid and liquid stimulants, artificial tastes, condiments—and these, in some of their various forms are partaken by all. By him who is determined to place his vigor and health above par, from his mouth and stomach, these must be rigidly excluded. Simple and hearty food, and no condiments, must be his motto. This too is the continual lesson of nature. By reason of it, we see that fine state of health which characterizes hunters, lumber- men, raftsmen, and sailors on shipboard. For in those situations the living is invariably coarse and solid, without delicacies. Of course, too, the open air and the habits of muscular exercise, must receive their due allowance. But are not exercise and the open air within the reach of us all?

In America, a great deal of the indigestion that prevails, is the result (we cannot too often recur to this) of a cause we have elsewhere alluded to, excessive mental action. Those who think much, or whose business cares return upon the mind, and are brooded over and over, are often, perhaps generally, the very men whose habit it is to eat copiously of rich viands, perhaps at the hotel table, and to deluge the stomach with liquids. How can anyone bear up under such inflictions, when the same person is probably the one who, week and week, and year after year, takes no systematic exercise, and does not know even what the training for health means?

Next week we shall go over the important question of when ought a man to be in his primmest condition, and how long? There will, we think, be some points in this matter that will be new to most of our readers.

CHAPTER 4

WHEN OUGHT A MAN BE IN HIS PRIMEST
CONDITION, AND HOW LONG?

PROBABLY WE SHALL surprise most of our readers by the answer to this question. According to the lives most of us lead, it is doubtful whether we are ever in that perfect state of health and strength that the human frame is capable of attaining, even without any special advantages— for, with most of us, all of the leading objects and aims we so eagerly pursue, bending time, energy, circumstances, everything, to their acquisition, this matter of health, strange as it may seem, is the one which surely receives the least consistent attention.

From about the twenty-fourth to near the fiftieth or fifty-fifth year, the body, in a fair specimen of health and condition, remains nearly stationary. The liability to disease is less, and all the powers are in their best working order. This is the period when a man makes his mark, if at all. Activity is now at its fullest; indeed, the repression or non-action of it, in many cases, is the greatest misfortune that can happen to this stage of life. All the labor and employments of the earth are served with these years—without them there would be little or nothing to show for man, for governments, for industry, for science, for civilization, literature or art.

It is during some portion of this stretch of time, varied in different persons, that all the celebrated men of the world have achieved the works which have given them renown. Some have started early, and finished, it may be said, prematurely; this is the case with many of the poets, especially those of passionate imagery and tone, such as the English celebrities, Shelley, Byron, Keats, etc. Of first-class works, however, it is doubtful whether any have ever yet been achieved by young men. Shakespeare wrote his best productions during the period from his thirty-seventh to his forty-fifth year.

When we ask how long a man ought to be in prime condition,

we, of course, mean how long, allowing a favorable state of care, habits, food, etc. With these, we deliberately say that if he have a fair natural constitution and has not ingrained his system in early life with the germs of any incurable malady, (this last is important—take notice young men!)—he ought to be in a high range of health and strength from the age of twenty-three or four years to the age of sixty-five—a space of over forty years. We know this is not in accordance with popular convictions on the subject; but, with great respect and good nature, we are fain to call this popular opinion by its true name, popular ignorance.

Take notice! however; if life, and its reserved fund of vitality, are dissipated during the years from fifteen to twenty-three or four—if extravagant and continued drains are made on the bodily stamina, during that period, we cannot promise any such result as that stated in the foregoing paragraph. The years from fourteen or fifteen to the age of twenty-four are the very ones, out of the whole stretch of life, when there is the most danger of breaking down the perfect tone of the body, not so much for the present, as for the future. What is done or left undone, at that period, returns again, after many years.

A word also to young men whose health has been injured, in dissipation. Even then the case is hardly bad enough, except in rare instances, to discourage any one who may read these lines from adopting a serious and (if he have strength of mind sufficient) unshakable resolution to acquire vigor and good condition—albeit the years between the fifteenth and twenty-fourth do present, in their reminiscences, some of the injurious facts we have alluded to. The human frame is full, in every case, of latent power. Though wounded, buffeted, violated, time and again, it seems joyously to respond to the first return of reason and natural habitudes. Indeed, of all the amazing things about the human body, one of the most amusing is, how much it can stand, and still live on!

We dwell upon this point a little, because, of our city readers there are but few young men who, with all the recklessness of their age, have not dipped to a greater or lesser depth into the so called pleasures of city life; few, indeed, but on whom regular habits, drink, artificial diet, late hours, and other characteristic marks nowadays, of having spent life in one of our great cities—and of indulgences there, still more lamentable in their effects upon the future health, stamina, and long life—have not left unmistakable remains. Fortunately, however, these young men we are speaking of are the very ones who, in general, have the greatest fund of natural vigor, and are able to throw off deleterious causes.

Such reliance do we make upon the last-mentioned item, that we feel disposed to include most of that large class of young men in our cities, who have "lived too fast," in our list of peaceful and encouraging probabilities. For them too are health and a sound tone, (at least in a great degree) if they persevere in the right means. Let it be clearly understood, however, that indulgences of perverted appetite, and violations of the laws of health, cannot go too long, with impunity. There will come a time when the turning point is reached. Our object is so to encourage the reader to realize what superior pleasure a good and natural state of health is, over all other gratifications that he will bring up on the right side of that point.

Yes, nature is more tolerant and bountiful than we supposed. Long injured and insulted, she yet keeps blessings in her hands, ready to be bestowed with freedom and certainty, on the first practical signs of repentance.

To return—let it be borne in mind, especially by parents, for their offspring's sake—let it be equally borne in mind by the youth, developing himself into early manhood—that the true plan of life involves a fine and robust condition of manhood, with every faculty of body and mind in full play and high health, from the twenty third or fourth year, on to beyond the sixtieth.

THE SURE REWARD

Is not all this something worth a young man's while to strive for, and lay out his plans for? We do not object to his careful and persistent regard for wealth, or for the objects of his business ambition, whatever they may be—but we say that nothing ought to displace the great pursuit we speak of—manly health and vigor. Even considered with reference to a far better capability of getting wealth, or of reaching the objects of ambition, health and strength are vitally important. With them, of course, not only so much more can be done, but the strain can be borne so much longer. From a money-making point of view, therefore, health is an investment that pays better than any other.

But we do not recommend the planning out of life by a young man, to realize this long-continued stretch of forty years of full health and strength, in order that he may make money. We recommend it for itself—its own interest, reward, and its manliness. For, say what we may of the pleasures of the world, and of what is heroic, it comes down to this—that there can be no first-rate heroism except in a sound body, and that there really can be no gratification or pleasure, however costly, however much vaunted or rare, or sought for, that is equal to the delicious feeling, all through middle-age, and even old age, of being perfectly well.

To spring up in the morning with light feelings, and the disposition to raise the voice in some cheerful song—to feel a pleasure in going forth into the open air, and in breathing it—to sit down to your food with a keen relish for it—to pass forth, in business or occupation, among men, without distrusting them, but with a friendly feeling toward all, and finding the same feeling returned to you—to be buoyant in all your limbs and movements by the curious result of perfect digestion, (a feeling as if you could almost fly, you are so light),—to have perfect command of your arms, legs, etc., able to strike out, if occasion demand, or to walk long distances, or to endure great labor without exhaustion to have year after year pass on and on, and still the same calm and equable state of all the organs, and of the temper and mentality—no wrenching pains of the nerves or joints—no pangs, returning again and again, through the sensitive head, or any of its parts—no blotched and disfigured complexion—no prematurely lame and halting gait—no tremulous shaking of the hand, unable to carry a glass of water to the mouth without spilling it—no film and bleared-red about the eyes, nor bad taste in the mouth, nor tainted breath from the stomach or gums—none of that dreary, sickening, unmanly lassitude, that, to so many men, fills up and curses what ought to be the best years of their lives, without good works to show for the same—but instead of such a living death, which, (to make a terrible but true confession) so many lead, uncomfortably realizing, through their middle age, more than the distresses and bleak impressions of death, stretched out year after year, the result of early ignorance, imprudence, and want of wholesome training—instead of that, to find life one long holiday, labor a pleasure, the body a heaven, the earth a paradise, all the commonest habits ministering to delight— and to have this continued year after year, and old age even, when it arrives, bringing no change to the capacity for a high state of manly enjoyment—these are what we would put before you, reader, as a true picture, illustrating the whole drift of our remarks, the sum of all, the best answer to the heading of the two last sections of our articles, and the main object which every youth should have, in the beginning, from the time he starts out to reason and judge for himself.

MODERN SOCIETY — EMPLOYMENTS

One great evil of most of the superficial advice on health and its conditions is that the writers do not consider, or have no patience with, the arbitrary lines and peculiarities of modern society, especially as it operates in the cities. Granted that many of these peculiarities are bad, it only remains to do the best that is possible under them. And if the thing is approached in this spirit, it will generally be found that most of the essential results can be attained without the violent standing out from, or opposition to the rest, which is impossible without much offense, and the giving up of much that conduces to prosperity, sociability and happiness.

Of the employments followed in the State of New York by the one million of grown, or nearly grown, males, 314,000 are of farming, gardening, or other agricultural pursuits; about 200,000 are laborers on various artificial works, in cities or elsewhere, (these are mostly of foreign birth); over 23,000 are sailors; 14,000 are lawyers, doctors, or ministers; 5,000 are office-holders; and 313,000 are mechanics, or engaged as operatives in some kind of manufactures—the rest being scattered through an immense number of small, or comparatively small, occupations. In general terms it may be stated that even in the United States, new and farming-country as it is, the number of those engaged in artificial pursuits is about equal to those engaged in agriculture.

How does all this affect the general health? The question is a profound one, and the conclusions in reference to it must not be jumped at too hastily. Close investigation, and the allowance of strict candor in statements, will perhaps prove that there is a good deal of popular error as to the necessary bad effects of manufacturing and other in-door employments upon individual health. We mean simply this, which a person, with anything like a decent or average physical constitution, can follow almost any of the usual avocations to be found in our cities, and still have a fine condition of health. If the latter is wanting, it is not so much the fault of the employment as of the person himself. Because civilization, with all its banes, and the ill health of masses, as before alluded to, has still more antidotes, if the choice were to be made between a life passed in the solitary freedom of barbarous and un-artificial nature, and the highly complicated, and, in many respects, morbid life of one of our modern cities, we think the preference might deliberately and safely be given to the latter, as more likely to confer not only a greater longevity, but a greater amount of average animal happiness; and singular as it may at first appear, the chances of the latter are in favor of a higher and more robust degree of health than the former. The former, with its freedom from the artificial evils, is bereft also of the means of favoring life, and improving it, which belong to the latter.

Modern society is distinguished for much that is artificial, no doubt. It is distinguished for labor-saving machinery, the mechanical arts, and for the number of human beings engaged in regular indoor employments. Of the grown men of the United States, about two millions earn their living and spend the best part of their lives in working at some trade, or in some factory, or in commerce, mining, etc. While some of these are partially conducive to health, from being more or less hardening, a vast majority are characterized by features that, under the ignorance of physiology which prevails, must be stamped as deleterious. It remains, we say, to still do the best we can under these circumstances. Nor is the case bad, as might be judged from merely pursuing the question thus far.

Nor in the various manufactures and trades is there anything which may not, in almost all cases, be partially or wholly obviated, and the health retained under them, year after year, by proper prudence and forethought. A man, for instance, engaged in work that gave him too little exercise in the open air, should accustom him-self, when not at work, to make up for that by out-door activity in some form or other—walking, or in some manly game. And this should not be occasional, but steady. Men whose occupation is partially active, but requires them to breathe close air, (as in many factories) might retrieve the matter greatly by having well-ventilated bed rooms. This is an important matter, to which we have elsewhere devoted a special paragraph. The reader must make for himself the application of these hints in his own case.

EARLY YOUTH STAMPS THE FUTURE PHYSIQUE

During childhood and youth much of the after-life receives its stamp and impression, for good or evil—especially the condition and power of growth of all the important functions and organs of the body. For American children it would be a great improvement if the food were more simple and digestible, instead of the hearty and seasoned dishes that are generally partaken alike by small and large. Another thing with regard to boys in the United States is that they far too soon commence all the indulgences of men, especially tobacco, drink, etc. While the system is being formed, and before the body has attained its growth and solidity, these ought to be forbidden indulgences.

From the age of fourteen to twenty one or two is a most important period, in the consideration of the health and vigor of a man with reference to the whole subsequent period of his life. Few youths consider the momentous results of all that is done, or left undone, during this part of their career. Parents, guardians, relatives, friends, are equally negligent. Otherwise, we should certainly see a far greater amount of influence directed toward this important class of persons, and their wellbeing.

We call upon those youths who read this to ponder, with all the strength and comprehension of their minds, upon what we are here trying to impress upon them—for they surely include some of the most important considerations that can be put before any human being, and come home directly to the experience of each one. Let every youth understand that it is mainly in his power, by

39

what he does or leaves undone, during the years we have mentioned to become a sound, healthy and handsome man, and remain so for many years, in full possession of his faculties and strength; or, failing in what leads to that result, to lay the early substrata of an early decay of vigor, a loss of all buoyancy of spirit, a broken and useless middle-age, and if not a premature death, an old age more miserable than death.

MANLY BEAUTY—THE TRUE AMBITION

We would here place before our readers, especially the youth, the thought that nothing is more worthy their ambition, and will surely repay the effort and resolution to follow them, than a steady pursuit of the regulations, laws, self-denials, and daily habitudes that lead to the sound condition and beautiful appearance of the body, the manly form—this wondrous and beautiful structure that never wearies the mind in contemplating its inward and outward mysteries, and in which, after all is said on other subjects, concentrates the whole interest of life, happiness, affection, dignity, and glory—around which, indeed, all history, all persons, and indeed all literature revolve, and find their sum and aggregate.

Reader! What is your ambition? We cannot, of course, tell; but one ambition, at any rate, you ought to have, and probably, while reading what we write, if never before, it will arise before you, more or less distinctly—and that is the desire and determination to put your body in a healthy and sweet-blooded condition—to be a man, hearty, active, muscular, handsome—yes, handsome—for it is not for nothing that all through the human race there is the universal desire that the body should not only be well, but look well. We would not give much for that man, young, middle-aged, or old, who was not touched by the feeling of pride or regret in his good or ill appearance. To one who has no such feeling, the electricity has gone out of that man; there is little hope for him. Nor is there anything to be ashamed of in the ambition of a man to have a handsome physique, a fine body, clear complexion, nimble movements, and be full of manly vigor. Ashamed of! Why, we think it ought to be one of the first lessons taught to the boy, when he begins to be taught at all. It is of quite as much importance as any grammar, geography, or arithmetic— indeed, we should say it was of unrivalled importance. Only let it be the ambition that realizes a masculine and robust style of beauty, not the beauty of parlor elegance, of too much refinement, or of the mere fop.

There is a little popular delusion on this subject which we would like to do our part toward dispelling. It is generally considered, or rather pretended to be considered, that personal beauty is something not proper for the attention of men, but must be left for the other sex. At the same time the instinct to take a pride in manly looks, as it can never be eradicated, is always more or less operative; and it is this that, taking nature for our guide, and always using the light of good sense and manly robustness and of judgment, we would act upon. We say, encourage American youth to develop and increase their physical beauty. How, then, can this be done? Much of it is to be looked for through a diffusion of more general information upon the subtle play of causes and effects, which make or unmake the health of the body. These often date back to early life, to causes that operate during the period from the thirteenth or fourteenth to the twenty-third or twenty-fourth year; and very many of our remarks, though applying to all ages, will specially apply to the period we have just named.

We repeat it, both for a prevalent application, and for the use of you, reader, who may be attracted to our well-meant paragraphs, be not afraid or ashamed definitely to make your physical beauty, of form, face and movement, a main point of interest you have here in life, at all of its periods, and whatever position of wealth or education you may be. It is a germ, implanted by nature that you should make grow. And out of it will come a prolific growth of good results, besides itself. It is a main part of that reception of friendship, admiration and good will which all desire, and which can always make life sweet.

CHAPTER 5

THE MAGNETIC ATTRACTION FROM HEALTH AND A MANLY PHYSIQUE CAN IT BE ATTAINED BY TRAINING?

OUR THEME COMMENDS itself further still. What do you suppose is the reason that some men have so much more power over the masses than other men?—such a "personality" that they can hardly appear in a crowd, or a room full of people, but their influence is felt? What is it at the bottom of the curious magnetism such men possess, and show it in house or street, in command, in the lecture-room, in the social circle, in politics, or on the field of battle? It is the subtle virtue of their physique—this just as much as intellect.

What we here affirm is proved by the fact that greater minds by far than any possessed by the commanding and magnetic persons we speak of, when clothed in inferior bodies, produce no effects at all, and come and go with the rest. A man of large personality, (it is not a matter of physical size—a small man may have it as well as any one) is probably one of the most interesting studies in the world, and one of the greatest exemplifications of our theory of man's vigor. There he is, an evidence of power, of health, of tone—registering all in his port, his carriage, the atmosphere of influence that effuses out of him whenever he moves.

It is indeed our theory, (and we call upon you, reader, to mark this, for it is well worth pondering upon) that a man of ordinary mental and physical advantages may, by training in its fullest sense, so exalt the intensity of his personal force, that virtue in him which utters itself at last through a perfect physique and a clear mind, that wherever he moves, in the private circle or in the crowd, he shall attract to him attention, friendship, and respect, openly or silently— one of the noblest proofs that can be given of what the body is capable of effecting!

Would you succeed in anything?—ambitious projects, business, love? Then cultivate this personal force, by persistent regard to the laws of health and vigor. And remember that the best successes of life are the general resultant of all the human attributes, expressed through a fine physique. This knowledge, this practice, you, too, reader, will need. All kinds of men, herculean, obstinate, petty, profound—men of oak and men of wax—meet you at every move, crowding and jostling through the by-ways of the world. These you would confront, you would command, would you not? At least, you would not be overborne by the proudest of them, but would hold your own on equal terms. Then observe our suggestions—train—acquire for yourself firm fibres, a stomach clear and capable, the brain-action un-abused, the stream of vital power full and voluminous, a bright eye, a strong voice, a proper degree of flesh, a transparent complexion—a fine average yet plus condition; and sympathy, attraction, and a heroic presence will follow. Are these trifles? Not a bit of it. They lie close to the heart of a man, and are among his secret, most cherished aspirations. With men, with women, with friends, with strangers, who is there that does not crave to be admired, to be beloved?

Is it not, indeed, worth striving for? Through a robust and clean-blooded physique, this personal attraction is the real means that must secure any object, and, in the long run, produce effects worth having, in society, in the popular assemblage, on the boards of the stage or the concert room, on the lecturer's platform, the political hall, addressing a jury, pleading a case with a fair damsel, or in the business relations of any buying and selling. All will succumb to it—all yield to its marvelous power.

This large potency, this subtle virtue of health and physique, we say, can be cultivated—it is hardly too much to say that it can be acquired; for we believe that, in almost every case, there are germs enough inherent in any man to work upon. But it will not be acquired except by him who perseveres and is faithful. Gluttony, sloth or inebriety must not even once be allowed to dull the perceptions, reverse the play and vigorous actions of the system—throwing the frame, and all its powers, prostrate, helpless, unable to show itself the master it would otherwise be.

This singular but sure magnetic condition, the result mainly of animal robustness, (through which the moral nature of course effuses) is, we cannot too often repeat, the result of the health of

43

the whole being, from top to toe—all must be sound, without exception—and then the stronger the tone of health, the mightier will be the stream of magnetic influence evolved. A main part doubtless lies in the department of sexuality; here a fund of vigor is a main part of a manly being, through many years; but he who exhausts himself, who commits excesses in youth, or becomes tainted in his blood, is attacked in the very citadel of manhood, and must pay the penalty through middle age, and the remaining periods of his life, as well as see the "attraction of personality" we have been speaking of depart from him.

In the department we speak of, a reserved stock of vital energy, we say, marks the man; and he who gives himself up, by its undue exhaustion, to lassitude and broken-down manhood, must bear the miserable consequences. The lesson is full of reflections, which we leave the reader to follow out.

Let a young man endeavor to realize of his body that, among other things, it is a machine calculated to produce force, an outpouring of subtle force, the same in moving among his fellow men as the orbs in space have in revolving through their orbits. Yes, a man, too, has his curious attraction of gravitation, and, well developed; it is one of the most amazing and delightful of natural results. This subject probably is new to you, reader, treated in this way; and yet if you will reflect a little, you will see that all history and real life in every direction abounds with illustrations of our statement.

What are most of the movements of men, all the past, whose signs we see around us, but assertions of what this human force has done—is now doing? Friendships, loves, some men well-liked wherever they go, others avoided or treated with indifference, the successful singer or actor, the orator that enchains his audience, the victory of the prize-fighter, the players of manly games, the person applauded in public, and the person whose efforts fall flat or are received with hisses of scorn or contempt—all these are just so many proofs of the powerful presence, or feeble absence, of the quality we are now treating of.

Observe the results of one day, to a man, at two different times, at a little distance from each other. He goes forth, neither feeling nor looking well; he has lived badly—his blood is bad—his joints move like those of some rusty machine, ill oiled—his eyes have red bloodshot in them—his complexion is muddied and pimpled—he is not clean, not having bathed for a long time—his stomach has been overloaded with all sorts of indigestible solids and injurious liquids. This has been going on so long that his digestion is seriously impaired—his bowels are clogged with accumulations of fearful impurity, like sewers that have been stopped—his gait is halting, and he would sit down often to rest—his appetite is morbid, seeking stimulants and spices to excess—the expression that beams from his face is anything but attractive—his breath is bad—nobody finds it a pleasure to be near him, or feels anything like delight from the magnetism of his voice, for there is no magnetism about it—he does not attract women, nor men either; and thus, going up and down, through the city, it may be, in the street, at table, wherever he moves, he is without vigor, with- out attraction, without pleasure, without force, without love, without independence, spirit or pride. Can there be a much sadder case? And is it by any means a rare one?

Now for another day—the same man—a little while, it may be but a few months, it need not be but a year at most, afterwards. Can this, indeed, be the result of the steady observance of a few physiological laws—the magic result of training? This day he rises with a merry song on his lips, and bounding strength in every muscle of his limbs. The shock of the cold-water bath in which he leaves his body is delicious to him—and the friction of the brush afterward tingles finely through the skin into his blood. Food, air, the simplest drink, every motion—all these give him pleasure. His eyes are bright and sparkling, his voice melodious and strong. As he goes forth among men, he is everywhere noticed, and draws toward him good-will and even envy. His walk is springy and elastic—his complexion pure—his attitude erect, his expression full of manliness, spirit, pride and a noble self-confidence. He has all the indescribable charm which belongs to some of the finest and most spirited animals, with flashing eyes, fine action, and unconquerable spirit, that we sometimes see in the brutes—but alas! Seldom see in the case of men. The full condition of power is attained by him—and the marvelous effects play invisibly out of him, wherever he moves, upon men and women in all directions.

45

Actors! vocalists! speakers! can you not here learn the secret of that coveted power over the public? a power as blessed to receive as it is to give.

To all, however, it is a great power—an art well worth the cultivation. Indeed, in the movements of common life, in the usual residence, and in company of acquaintances and friends—there we should say would be found its most grateful spheres of operation—for there the happiness of life, in the man, must rest.

BIRTH-INFLUENCES — BREEDING SUPERB MEN

It is a profound reflection, deeply intertwined with our subject, that much of a man's comfort or discomfort, body and mind, depends on causes that exist and operate, in full activity, before his birth; these are the long train of hereditary causes that cannot too frequently be recurred to and dwelt upon. The laws of transmission of qualities, tendencies and forms, from parents to offspring, have always been among the most perplexing, as well as fascinating studies of the physician. The reasons of such transmission will doubtless continue to remain unexplained—the facts are innumerable, and run even deeper and farther backward and forward than is generally supposed. Unfortunately, however, there has never yet been found a generation that would shape its course, or give up any of its pleasures, for the greater perfection of the generation which was to follow.

While we cannot resume the past, however, in considering the health, size, looks, strength, etc., of a full-grown man—his beauty and perfection in those points, or his deficiency in them—it may be useful, for future cases, at any rate, to consider that whatever the man is, results, in a great degree, from those hereditary causes —causes that were in operation before he was born. Parentage! how great a thing it is! How the whole subject of life, of race, of temper, etc., all date back, without possibility of escape, to parentage! Yet it is not the future only that is involved—the present also comes in for consideration, as much as that.

Because the same routine of law, causes and effects, that operate to produce sound offspring, and perpetuate health, growth, vigorous maturity and long life in the same, are the identical laws, causes and effects that, by their interplay, have to do with a perfect

46

physique in the parent. If only for the good of the latter, those laws are indispensable. They are the very ones that go to make the youth, the grown person, the middle-aged, strong and sound. So that to be in the condition of true parentage, or of preparing to be, is only another phrase for being in the true condition for yourself, and for all that makes you a true specimen of a man.

Mothers, too, it is useless to deny, are, for the main part, sadly unaware of most of the best conditions of treatment, food, etc., that lay the foundation, in early childhood and youth, for future manliness and a fine physique. So true is this, so lamentably true, that, beyond a doubt, if the mothers of the young children of this, or any other generation, were to put in practice, and carry out through the years of infancy and childhood, the simplest laws of sound physiology, and form the young into the habits thereof, we should see an entirely different and immeasurably superior race of men advancing upon the earth.

In the scope of our articles on health, we do not include the full statement of this most important and interesting part of our topic. It deserves, from every one, far more conscientious examination than is usually given to it. No considerations of morbid modesty should be allowed to stand in the way; and indeed, are not those the immodest ones who would prohibit the enlightenment of the world, both men and women, grown and un grown, upon what is so vital to them, and to all who come after them—prohibit it from prurient suspicions that it cannot be examined and investigated (as it certainly can be) with the noblest intentions, and in the most manly and even religious spirit?

While, therefore, it does not fall within the line of our remarks here to expatiate upon the laws of hereditary descent, and of parentage—the science, it might be called, of breeding superb men and women—we enjoin upon the reader to study out those laws, and what they result it. To know them is often to be forewarned with some of the most valuable knowledge it is possible for a man to have. He is able, then, to judge of much in his own case that, without which, would be dark and puzzling to him. He is a l s o able to act understandingly toward the future.

We think proper to add, that we include women just the same as men, in the foregoing remarks.

LONG LIFE AND ITS REQUISITES

We have always had a great curiosity, and felt an interest in cases of extreme old age. Returning from the west a couple of seasons since, we made a detour from our regular course to visit an aged woman, who numbered 103 years, and yet was in perfectly good condition, and retained her mental faculties unimpaired. This lady was Mrs. Catherine Dunn, of Nunda, in this State. She stated that she had always been very healthy and strong—altogether a pleasing and remarkable case.

One of the most noted cases of strength and faculty in old age is that of the old chaplain of the House of Representatives, at Washington, Rev. Daniel Waldo, who is between 95 and 100. He has been preaching for three quarters of a century—was a chaplain in the Revolutionary army, and was confined in the celebrated "Sugar House" prison in New York City. This aged man has always followed quite an active life, and has never been sick; living, for many years, on his farm near Syracuse. He keeps up with the times, too, reads all the new books, and is eager as anyone to hear the latest news—quite a young old man.

Among the curious cases mentioned by Lord Bacon in his work on the "Prolongation of Life" are many of ancient date, among the Greeks, Asiatics, etc. Among the latter, the Essenes a sect of Jews, are said to have very commonly attained the age of a hundred years; it was attributed to their great temperance in diet, and to a calm habit of mind which they cultivated. As one of various specimens presented by Lord Bacon, we give the following:—Apollonius Tyaneus exceeded a hundred years, his face betraying no such age; he was an admirable man of the heathens, reputed to have something divine in him, of the Christians held for a sorcerer—in his diet, Pythagorical—a great traveler, much renowned, and by some adored as a god; and lest his long life should be attributed to his vegetable diet, his grandfather before him, who did not restrict himself, lived to a hundred and thirty years. The two next cases, quaintly related in the style of that time, are also from Lord   Bacon's work: Most memorable is that of Cornarus, the Venetian, who, being in his youth of a sickly body, began first to eat and drink by measure to a certain weight, thereby to

48

recover his health; this cure turned by use into a diet, and that diet to an extraordinarily long life, even of a hundred years and better, without any decay of his senses, and with a constant enjoying of his health. In later times, William Pestel, a Frenchman, lived to a hundred and well-nigh twenty years, the top of his beard on his upper lip being black; a man of a fancy not altogether sound, but somewhat crazed in his brain—a great traveler, mathematician, and somewhat stained with heresy.

About twelve years ago there was living in the town of Frankford, near Utica, a man by the name of Harvey, 111 years of age. He, too, had been for three-fourths of a century a preacher of the gospel. From an informant who saw him at that time, we learned that he was born in Dutchess County, N. Y., and that he distinctly remembered running about there in the woods a hundred years ago! During his life he had devoted some of his time and attention to farming, but always preached—and was doing so when we heard of him! He walked without any assistance, except that of a staff. His conversation, as well as his style of preaching, was animated—and frequently his eye brightened with the vivacity of youth. His mind appeared to be clear and sound, and his voice was strong enough to be heard through an assemblage of a thousand persons, or more. Wherever he went, multitudes flocked to hear him.

The same informant, (an amateur in the study of longevity) gives us an account of Mrs. Hannah Gough, who died in New York City in 1846, at the age of 110 years. She had always resided in New York, and had seen and conversed with every President of the United States. This case is interesting, as one of not a few that prove the city capable of conferring life as well as the country.

In cold climates, it is probable that persons are apt to live to a greater age than in tropical ones, or those toward the tropics. The climate of the Northern States, especially through New England, is favorable to longevity. We have gleaned the following from a long list of authenticated instances: A Mrs. Blake dies in Portland, Maine, in 1824, aged 112 years; Mrs. Moody died the same year, aged 111; John Gilley died in Augusta, Maine, 1813, aged 124; Morris Wheeler, in Readfield, Maine, in 1817, aged 115. Other Eastern states afford still more numerous instances, which we need not specify. The middle states are also full of specimens of great longevity.

One of the oldest persons of whom we have any record in this or any country was Betsey Tranthram, who died in Tennessee in 1834, aged 154 years! A Negro died in Pennsylvania in 1808, aged 150. While we write this, we hear accounts of an aged lady in the District of Columbia, supposed to be 150 years of age; she had had ten children previous to the commencement of the Revolutionary war.

Indeed, in all directions, in modern times just the same as any, there are plenty of instances to prove that human life may last for a century and over, and remain in pretty good condition then. It is very much to be desired that someone should collect in a volume these cases of great longevity, and the peculiarities of them.

It being thus settled beyond a doubt that, under fair conditions, the human frame is capable of a far greater endurance than is generally supposed—that the number of persons in different parts of the earth, who have long outlived the "seventy years" allotted to man, may be numbered not by dozens merely, but by hundreds, and probably thousands—it remains to inquire into the causes that have led to such a result, and give heed to it, as a most precious lesson. Not so much that long livers have remained such a great while upon the earth, as that they must have had a good and sound life.

It will be found in all cases of these long livers, that they did not exhaust the stamina of the frame in their adolescent years, the years from fourteen to twenty-three or four. During this important period of their lives, nature was left to grow strong, harden itself, and strike its roots deep—the whole system being daily prepared for all future emergencies. For it is idle to suppose of the long-livers we allude to, but that they also had their ills, troubles, losses, and the various fortunes that beset, at times, every human being in his journey through this world. But if the body once attains its wholesome growth and solidity, without having the germs of decay infused through it while the juices of life are yet green, it can stand an immense strain upon it afterward without harm. We would impress this as the most important of the many lessons of manly development, health, and the continuance of life.

It is like a house perfect in the foundation, which then needs but the ordinary repairs, and will keep lasting an indefinite period of time. But the foundation shaky or insecure, it may be patched and mended forever, and still at any moment be liable to serious overthrow or damage.

REGULAR OCCUPATION

A steady and agreeable occupation is one of the most potent adjuncts and favorers of health and long life. The idler, without object, with- out definite direction, is very apt to brood himself into some moral or physical fever—and one is about as bad as the other.

Disappointment, love, business troubles, and a long list of dark possibilities, are always waiting around every man; these interact, when they happen, (and none can go through life without them) in many ways upon the health. When they do happen, it is no excuse for "giving up"; if one will only persevere in the wholesome observances, and patiently wait a few days, the mind will be again at ease, and spring up with cheerful vigor again. This is one of the greatest recommendations of the training system, which, if our advice could be followed by young men, we would have never intermitted through life. It would be their best armor for all the ills that would be likely to beset them; to others baffling and overcoming, but to them obstacles easily turned aside and traveled away from.

VEGETABLE DIET

We neither practice the vegetarian system ourselves, nor do we recommend it to others as anything like what its enthusiastic advocates claim it to be; and yet we think vegetarianism well worth a respectful mention. From the most ancient times, the system has come down to us under the most venerable authority. Nearly all of the early philosophers and saints appear to have been men who observed this diet; and, it must also be said, nearly all of them obtained a very advanced period of life. In the

51

remarks elsewhere given on longevity, the cases mentioned, as near as can be authenticated, made use of that kind of aliment altogether, or nearly altogether. Newton, the astronomer, it is well known, in his profound and intricate discoveries, sometimes occupying his powers for weeks and months at a time, lived on vegetable food, and drank water only; thus forming a habit from which he seldom departed, and attaining to his eighty-fifth year. Boyle, the great chemist, although of extremely delicate constitution, by the simplicity and regularity of living, abstaining from animal food, and also by drinking nothing but water, preserved his useful life far beyond all expectation, dying in his sixty-sixth year —where most others would, in all probability, not have attained to half that age.

We recollect reading in an old book of travels a description by the traveler, of the head official of a Spanish convent of monks, an aged man, who had always lived upon vegetable food, and whose drink had been water only. He wore, says our traveler, a large garment of coarse cloth, tied at the waist with a rope, and having a hood for his head; and on his feet coarse shoes of half-tanned leather. Yet there was something in his appearance which would have enabled one to single him out at once from a whole fraternity. He had a lofty and towering form, and features of the very noblest mould. His beard descended low upon his breast, and was partly hid in the folds of his dress. The man was one who in any spot would attract attention, but as he stood there at the entrance of his convent, in addition to the effect of his apostolic garment, his complexion and his eye had a clearness that no one can conceive who is not familiar with the aspect of those who have practiced a long and rigid abstinence from animal food, and from every exciting aliment. It gives a lustre, a spiritual intelligence to the countenance, that has something saint-like and divine.

This is, of course, a little enthusiastic. We have seen New England and New York vegetarians, gaunt, hard, melancholy, and unhappy looking persons, that looked like anything else than a recommendation of their doctrine—for that is the proof, after all.

CHAPTER 6

STUDY OF THEORIES OF HEALTH

ONE OF THE greatest mistakes made in arbitrary theories of certain things supposed to be conducive to health, is that they forget that the true theory of health is multiform, and does not consist of one or two rules alone. The vegetarian, for instance, insists on the total salvation of the human race, if they would only abstain from animal food! This is ridiculous. Others have their hobbies — some of one kind, some of a different. But it is often to be noticed that, in the same person, habits exist that mutually contradict each other, and are parts of opposite theories.

A system of health, in order to be worth following, ought to be consistent in all its parts, and complete besides; and then followed faithfully for a long time. It is too much to expect any great immediate results; it is quite enough if they come in the course of a few months. It is also to be understood that every man's case requires something especially applicable to it.

We should recommend any one to first get a general knowledge of the subject, through what has been written upon it, without, for a while, undertaking to examine every branch minutely. It is a study, moreover, which will grow upon one, and as its illustrations lie within the daily experience of us each and all, it can be continually pursued.

EXERCISES, GAMES, AND OFF-HAND CONTRIVANCES

The game of Baseball, now very generally practiced, is one of the very best of out-door exercises; the same may be said of cricket—and, in short, of all games which involve the using of the arms and legs.

Rowing is a noble and manly exercise; it develops the whole of the body. To many, the hunter's excursion, with dog and gun, will prove salutary. The fishing jaunt the same.

"Hurling" is also a noble game, and calculated, if made popular, to help with the rest in producing a noble race of men. We happened, by accident, to be present at a game of this sort, a few days since, in Brooklyn. The preliminaries being arranged (it was in a fine, large, enclosed lot) the hurlers stripped, and with hurl-bat in hand awaited the throwing up of the ball. The latter flew high in the air amidst the silence of the crowd, which, as the ball received the first "puck," broke into a loud cheer. Once in motion, an exciting struggle commenced, in which the greatest strength, skill and activity were exhibited, this continued for nearly three hours. This was our first observation of the practical working of the game, but from what we saw of it we can recommend it as worth a high place on a list of manly exercises.

The simplest performance of hurling, however, as the name imports, is merely throwing a heavy weight, often a large stone, or a blacksmith's or stone-cutter's sledge—each person trying to outdo the rest in the distance the sledge or stone is sent. Nor do we know a better exercise than this. It should hold its place in all the programs of work to be done.

Quoits—We wish this graceful and ancient game were more common. There is far more "science" in it than is generally supposed. In former ages, before the invention of gunpowder, when missiles were used in warfare, the lessons of this game were in vogue to give adroitness and precision in throwing objects with the arm. By a practiced player, almost any mark can be hit. Boys should be encouraged to play the game. In country places it is often played with flat stones, or with horse-shoes. Most of our American cities have grounds where it is regularly played.

In truth, however, a man who is disposed to attend to the matter of strengthening and developing his muscular power, will be continually finding some means to further that object, and will do so in the simplest manner, as well as any. To toss a stone in the air from one hand and catch it in the other as you walk along, for half an hour or an hour at a stretch—to push and roll over, a similar length of time, some small rock with the foot, thus developing the strength of the knees and the ankles and muscles of the calf—to throw forward the arms, with vigorous motion, and then extend them or lift them upward—to pummel some imaginary foe, with stroke after stroke from the doubled fists, given with a will—to place the body in position occasionally, for a moment, with all the sinews of the arms and legs strained to their utmost tension—to take very long strides rapidly forward, and then, more slowly and carefully, backward—to clap the palms of the hands on the hips and simply jump straight up, two or three minutes at a time—to stand on a hill or shore and throw stones, sometimes horizontally, sometimes perpendicularly — to spring over a fence, and then back again, and then again and again—to climb trees in the woods, or gripe the low branches with your hands and swing backward and forward—to run, or rapidly walk, or skip or leap along—these, and dozens more of simple contrivances, are at hand for every one—all good, all conducive to manly health, dexterity, and development, and, for many, preferable to the organized gymnasium, because they are not restricted to place or time. Nor let the reader be afraid of these because they are simple, but form the daily habit of some of them, without making himself uneasy "how it will look" to outsiders, or what they will say.

STRENGTH OF THE LEGS AND FEET

Much, very much, ought to be said on this subject. Walking, or some form of it, is nature's great exercise—so far ahead of all others as to make them of no account in comparison. In modern times, and among all classes of people, the cheap and rapid methods of traveling almost everywhere in vogue, have certainly made a sad depreciation in the locomotive powers of the race.

Of the persistent exercise, for strengthening and developing them, of the lower legs, and of the ankles and feet, very much might also be said. No example is yet seen—not in these days, hereabout, at least— of the quality of endurance and performance by the legs—walking, running, leaping, supporting, etc. (We suppose there are some who will dissent from us; but that is our deliberate opinion.) The legs have a great deal to do with the accomplishment of the work of the other parts of the body, and give grace and impetus to it all.

It is a singular fact that what might be supposed such a simple accomplishment as perfect and graceful walking, is very rare—is hard- ly ever seen in the streets of our cities. We have plenty of teachers of dancing—yet to walk well is more desirable than the

55

finest dancing. Perhaps some of the teachers we allude to might take a hint from the foregoing paragraph.

A great deal may be done by gymnastic exercises to increase the flexibility and muscular power of the legs. The ordinary exercise of bending forward and touching the toes with the tips of the fingers, keeping the knees straight meanwhile, is a very good one, and may be kept on with, in moderation at a time, for years and years. The simple exercise of standing on one foot and lowering so as to touch the bent knee of the other leg to the ground, and then rising again on the first foot, is also a good one. On the exercise ground, a good result is obtained from having a large stone and pushing or rolling it over, first by one foot, and then by the other, as long as it can be done without fatigue.

The art of the dancing-master may also be called in play, for the development of the legs, and their graceful and supple movement. As originally intended, dancing was meant to give harmonious movements to the whole body, from the legs, by keeping time to music. In that sense, it was a beautiful art, and one of the noblest of gymnastic exercises. Modern arrangements have made it something quite different.

We would be glad to see some manly genius arise among the dancing teachers, who, out of such hints as we have hastily written, would assist the objects of the trainer and gymnast.

SWIMMING AND BATHING

Many advantages are here concentrated in one—for swimming, being relieved of all the clothes, and supported in the water, allows of bringing nearly all the muscles of the body into easy and pleasant action. Persons habituated to a daily summer swim, or to the rapid wash with cold water over the whole body in the water, are far less liable to sudden colds, inflammatory diseases, or to the suffering of chronic complaints. The skin, one of the great inlets of disease, becomes tough and thick, and the processes of life are carried on with much more vigor. Then cleanliness and enjoyment are also to be added to the merits of swimming.

Where swimming is not eligible, then bathe. The tonic and sanitary effects of cold water are too precious to be foregone in some of their forms. You cannot have a manly soundness, unless the pores of the skin are kept open, and encouragement given to the insensible perspiration, which in a live man is thrown off in great quantities, and the free egress of which is of the utmost importance.

Even the first shock, the reviving chill of the cold water, will soon come to be welcome. On a hot day, how refreshing to feel the cool liquid poured over the naked body—or even dashed upon the face, head, hands and wrists. Cheap and simple as it is, there is a pleasure about it which costly enjoyments might not give.

We hear much, now-a-days, of the Water-Cure; but the real merit of the habitual use of water, especially swimming in it, is to prevent illness—in which it has a far greater scope. Buoyed up on the liquid element, the body of the swimmer is supported by an equal pressure on every part—none of the limbs and joints are overstrained, and none relaxed. It is probably one of the most ancient of health generating and body-perfecting exercises. The sculptors say that the ample development which the muscles, trunk, lungs, etc., obtained in the regular swimming, (in the open waters, or the large baths) of the Greeks and Romans, gave their chests that round and full form so noticeable in their statues.

Probably the finest and best developed forms now to be found in any portion of the human race are those of the South Sea Islanders, who bathe in the sea continually, and are as much at home there as on the land; and where the diseases of civilization have not been introduced, it is rare to find among them a case of sickness, deformity, or decrepitude—and hardly a death, except from extreme old age.

In learning to swim, which should be in childhood—but at no age is it too late—the main thing is to keep going in the water, once every day in summer, in a place not deep, and in moving around, and occasionally trying to strike out a little. The art will soon come to one who does this.

Early in the morning, in summer, is a good time to swim, or take a basin-wash; the evening is also good for either. Avoid going into the water immediately after a meal; and, also, do not stay in too long— never long enough to get chilled. We do not mean by this latter the cool feeling of the first shock, after which there is a reaction, and the system soon, by the exercise, becomes all aglow—but the blue and trembling chill of exposing the naked body to a low temperature too long, especially if not accompanied by active motion of the limbs, rubbing, etc. Stop while the warmth continues, give the whole body a brisk friction and drying, and the good effects will be permanent.

It is somewhat remarkable, and equally to be regretted, that we Americans, in every part of our land, are not a nation of swimmers; although our cost of sea, bay, and inlet includes thousands of miles, and lakes, rivers, creeks, ponds, etc., are profusely distributed in every state and every county. To this, among other causes, is to be assigned our too frequently gaunt, bilious and non-perfect national physique. Certain it is, to our mind, that the popular commencement and introduction of the habit of daily swimming, which, in four-fifths of the United States, need hardly be intermitted more than from three to four months in the year, would not only be great reform in itself, but would carry with it, and cause to rise out of it, many of the other practices that complete the human form, and make it what it ought in general to be, large, clean, beautiful, and long-lived—instead of that being the marked exception, as at present.

If the reader, either a young or middle-aged man, should be induced by our remarks to commence learning to swim, or the practice of washing the body, let him (as in all new things of this sort) commence with moderation, and be satisfied to form the habit by degrees—not giving up, however, because of some little personal discomfort, or inconvenience of any kind, at first. Even in such a habit as bathing, to a novice, a good deal of resolution and perseverance is needed; but after the habit is once formed, it will almost invariably be kept up, of a man's own accord.

After washing the body, the use of dry cloths, to rub the flesh briskly, is almost always to be observed. An animated walk afterwards will come in well.

TRAINING THE VOICE

The voice can be cultivated, strengthened and made melodi-ous, with an ease and certainty, and to degrees of which very few people have any notion. We do not know a better exercise, either for young or middle-aged men, than practicing (at first with moderation), in loudly reciting and declaiming in the open air, or in some large room. This should be systematic and daily; it strengthens and develops all the large organs, opens the chest, and not only gives decision and vigor to the utterance, in common life, and for all practical purposes, but has a most salutary effect on the throat, with its curious and exquisite machinery, hardening it all, and making it less liable to disease. It helps, indeed, the bodily system in many ways—gives a large inspiration and respiration, provokes the habit of electricity through the frame, plays upon the action of the stomach, and gives a dash and style to the personality of a man.

We would recommend every young man to select a few favorite poetical or other passages, of an animated description, and get in the habit of declaiming them, on all convenient occasions—especially when out upon the water, or by the sea-shore, or rambling over the hills on the country. Let him not be too timid or bashful about this, but throw himself into it with a will. Careful, however, not to overstrain his voice, or scream, for that is not the object that is aimed after. A loud, slow, firm tone, as long as it can be sustained without fatigue, and agreeably to the ear, is the test. Some voices will need to be used with great care for a long while. For in this, too, as in all physical exercises, let the learner remember, that there is plenty of time, and that it is the habit we mainly wish to form; after which the results will be sure to come in good time. We repeat emphatically, that all persons whose life or occupation requires the frequent use of the vocal organs, and makes a fine, clear tone, and a superior pronunciation desirable, (as to what human being is it not?) may greatly aid the production of that tone and pronunciation, by exercise, by habituating themselves to open the mouth, by carefully avoiding all nasal and other unpleasant habits, and by regular attention to the health, especially in the way of simplicity of food.

NOT TOO VIOLENT EXERCISE

Though we have once or twice alluded to the great importance of steady, daily, moderate exercise, as better than any extreme taxing of the bodily powers, at intervals, we think it of sufficient weight to call attention to it in a special paragraph.

The great object is to have the body in a condition of strong equilibrium—but very violent exertions defeat this end. In youth, or for young men, we may mention the evils of undue exertion, lifting immense weights, overworking in the fields of a long and hot day, being badly strained or wrenched in wrestling, or excessive and ill-timed "run" (as often happens to young firemen in our cities) as some of the occasions when the results we deprecate are apt to take their rise.

We would over and over again caution the young reader of our articles of the often incurable effects of some of these brief but excessive outlays of strength. The fund of vigor and stamina must be used constantly, and encouraged to develop itself gently, but never violently abused.

In training exercises, as before remarked, begin and keep on for a few days with great moderation. "Gently does it," is the motto which must never be forgotten. The custom among some young men of trying to perform very difficult and dangerous feats should be discouraged. These are only for the professional gymnasts, who have made them the study of their lives. Nor are any of those feats worth applauding unless they are evidently performed with ease.

GYMNASTIC SCHOOLS

It is very desirable that these should become common through our cities—some for beginners, young boys, etc., and others for grown persons, and those who have attained sufficient strength and endurance. Because the exercises for young boys should continue to be moderate, and gradually advance from the easier ones— taking particular care, in the spirit of the charge previously given, not to attempt feats of any kind merely because they are very difficult. This, indeed, in all gymnastic schools for boys, ought to be a sufficient reason to exclude any feat or exercise.

OUT-DOORS

In that word is the great antiseptic—the true medicine of humanity. We have confessed in our articles that there is no withstanding the modern requirements of life, which compel myriads of men to pass a great portion of the time employed in confined places, factories and the like; and that, this being accepted, the health and vigor of the body must be carried to a high pitch, and can be. Still, it is to be understood that, as a counterweight to the effects of confined air and employment, much, very much reliance is to be placed on inhaling the air, and in walking, or otherwise gently exercising, as much as possible out-doors. We have elsewhere mentioned the formation of the habit of walking; this is to be one of the main dependencies of the in-door employee. It does not tire, like other exercises—but, with practice, may be continued almost without limit.

Few know what virtue there is in the open air. Beyond all charms or medications, it is what renews vitality, and, as much as the nightly sleep, keeps the system from wearing out and stagnating upon itself. Naturally, we should all breathe this health-bestowing fluid; but the thousand artificial forms and necessities prevent it. We must, there- fore, do the best we can—first understanding what sustenance to the blood there is in the air, even to the remedying of the evils of the great portion of our lives that we are debarred from it.

Places of training, and all for gymnastic exercises, should be in the open air—upon the turf or sand is best. Cellars and low-roofed attics are to be condemned, especially the former.

EARLY RISING

The habit of rising early is not only of priceless value in itself, as a means toward, and concomitant of health, but is of equal importance from what the habit carries with it, apart from itself. In nature, there is no example of the bad practice of an animal, in full development of health and strength, in fine weather, lingering in its place of rest, nerveless and half dead, for hours and hours after the sun has risen. The only thing like it is the torpid condition of some animals, mostly in the Arctic and Antarctic regions, during the depth of the winter season. But civilized life, with its closed houses, its fires for warmth, and its plentiful and cheap envelopment of clothing, is protected against winters, and makes any copying of such an example unnecessary.

Summer and winter, he who intends to have his physique in good condition must rise early. This is an immutable law. It is one of the most important points of thorough training, and is to be relied on as much as anything else.

It is worth noting that the law of rising early necessitates the habit of retiring to bed in good season, which cuts off many of the dissipations most injurious in their effects upon the health. So important is this, that he who should adopt this rule alone will go a great way toward a complete reform—if reform be needed.

We will hardly reach our assertions to the extravagant length of some of the lauders of the habit of early rising—those, for instance, who hold to the celebrated maxim of Franklin, we believe, who said: "No great work can be performed, and no person can ever be good or great, without early rising." We are of those who believe that no law is without exceptions; and there may, after all, be aims, in which the health, for the time being, has to stand aside and take its chances. But, for a perfect attainment of that aim, namely, health and a fine physique, we may candidly say that we do not believe it can be accomplished at all without the habit we speak of.

NIGHT-EATING

An eccentric but wise old country physician, down in the state of Georgia, who was himself a living example of good health and unimpaired faculties, used to have a saying about people's meals, to the following purport: "Eat a good breakfast if you can, a good dinner if you will, but no supper if you please." In city life, and very largely among all classes, the spirit of the foregoing aphorism is exactly reversed; very few eating any breakfast—being without appetite for that meal, while the late hour of a fashionable dinner makes it equivalent to an evening feast. And then the habits of modern society invite to more or less indulgence of the appetite afterwards.

We allude to the custom of all modern amusements being held in the evening—parties, balls, theatres, concerts, etc. A main part of these, or an invariable accompaniment of them, are suppers, generally rich ones. Some of these are at 11, 12 or 1 o'clock at night, when numbers of people gorge themselves with hearty viands, oysters, jellies, beefsteaks, poultry, and more or less out of the hundreds of condiments, creams, and drinks.

A gentle and moderate refreshment at night is admissible enough; and, indeed, if accompanied with the convivial pleasure of friends, the cheerful song, or the excitement of company, and the wholesome stimulus of surrounding good fellowship, is every way to be commended.

But it must be borne in mind that, as a general thing, the stomach needs rest as much as the other parts of the system—as much as the brain, the hands, or the feet. The arrangements of every individual, for his eating, ought to be so prepared, if possible, as to make his appetite always possess keenness and readiness in the morning. There is not a surer sign that things are going wrong than that which is indicated by no want or relish for food, soon after rising, or in the early part of the day.

Portions of heavy food, or large quantities of any kind, taken at evening, or any time during the night, attract an undue amount of the nervous energy to the stomach, and give an overreaction to the feelings and powers, which is sure to be followed the next day by more or less bad reactionary consequences; and, if persevered in, must be a strong constitution indeed which does not break down.

Somebody has said that "we dig our graves with our teeth." There is a great deal of exaggerated statement about the evils of hearty eating, (we mean of plain food) — but it is very true that this habit we are complaining of, and endeavoring to guard the reader against, habitual night-eating, quite justifies the proverb. In this, as in all other instances, nature must be considered, and must decide before all artificial decisions. If there be those whose employments, or combinations of circumstances beyond their control, make it imperative upon them to violate the natural rules of eating, those persons must then make up for such violations by temperance, regularity and extra care in all other respects. They must choose with invariable prudence the quality of their food, simple and digestible dishes, and be as abstemious as possible. Actors and actresses, public performers, writers and printers on morning newspapers, pressmen, persons of the ferries, the city cars, and a numerous body of operatives and others, under modern arrangements, are all deeply involved in the bearings of this matter. In nearly all such and the like cases, a great and salutary improvement could be made in their comfort and health by a little prudent regard for their hours of eating and choice of aliment, and by bringing both as near to the standard of nature and simplicity as possible.

CHAPTER 7

THAT WE USE far too many stimulating drinks has been too long the burden of physicians and others to make the statement anything new to our readers. But we believe, for all that, the prevailing impression has hardly been turned in the right direction. We think that water, tea, coffee, soda, lemonade, "slops" of all sorts, have also produced, and are producing, immense injury to the health of the people—from their being used in too great quantities and at wrong times.

It may sound strange that so harmless a liquid as water may require to be guarded against, but it is even so. Drenching the stomach with it just before, or during a hearty meal, plays the mischief with the digestions, and in most cases with the personal comfort. And yet it is a common practice.

We are fain to say, also, that very much of the violent crusade of modern times against brewed and distilled liquors is far from being warranted by the true theory of health, and of physiological laws, as long as those liquors are not partaken of in improper quantities and at injudicious times, disturbing the digestion. Of the two, indeed, we would rather, a little while after his dinner, a man should drink a glass of good ale or wine than one of those mixtures called "soda," or even a strong cup of hot coffee.

We mention this, not as recommending any of those drinks to whoever, young, old, or middle-aged, is in pursuit of health and a manly physique, but by comparison. The drink we recommend, and not too much of that, is water only.

By a proper choice of food, much thirst may always be avoided. For it is mostly from using great quantities of salted, and other thirst-provoking food, (also the use of tobacco) that causes the imbibing of immense quantities of liquids used by our American men. About three-quarters of the drink is decidedly deleterious also, leaving afterward some of the various ingredients held in solution by the liquor, as a deposit in the stomach. Disguised, sweetened, & etc., many a dose of semi-poison is taken in the shape of a pleasant drink.

Then of hot drinks—if you are disposed, indeed, to place your physique in perfect condition, it is probable that you must give these up entirely. In almost all cases, they are enervating, injure the action of the stomach upon the food, and produce bad effects upon the general tone of the system. Under present arrangements, at the tables of hotels, boarding-houses, and indeed everywhere, the supply of hot coffee, tea, cocoa, etc., is largely drawn upon twice a day; some drinking two cups, some three, at a meal. The result of thus deluging the stomach with liquid in large quantities, and at a high temperature, is bad, in more ways than one. Besides the injuries previously named, it really prevents the appetite from craving wholesome food at the time. This is contrary to the general supposition, but it is true. At a meal, a man must not fill himself with a quantity of hot liquid, because he has no appetite for solid aliment; it were preferable that he should eat a little of some dish that is on the table, or even a crust of dry bread, a cracker or two, or something of that kind. Be it remembered, however, that we are not disposed to be extra rigid in the matter; if one enjoys coffee or tea, one moderate cup, not hot, and taken toward the end of the meal, to moisten the articles we have just advised, need not be too strenuously prohibited. It is only that we speak with candor to those who are determined to have the condition of health we have spoken of—who realize it as a prize worth striving for, and who will not let any gratifications of the palate stand in the way.

Hot drinks, however, are so much matters of habit that it only needs a little self-denial and perseverance for a week or two, to acquire an easy way of getting along without them—of seeing them placed before you, and quietly abstaining from them yourself while you see others use them. Such things may be called trifles; but if anyone wants to show his strength of mind, and ability to control himself, and prove what of back-bone and stamina there is in him, let him try his hand at giving supreme sway over reason, in sternly deciding to abstain from these very trifles.

Nature, it would seem, is averse to either very hot or very cold drinks or aliment. They should, in general, be as near as possible to the temperature of the body. As to the appetite for ice-water, for instance, in the hot weather, it is an artificial one; simple cool water, and not too cool, is much more wholesome.

MEDICINES—DO THEY DO ANY GOOD?

It is probable that the people of the United States use more medicines than any other equal number of persons in the world. In our cities, in all the main streets there is a drug-store to be seen every two or three blocks—and we know of some of the streets of New York and Brooklyn, where, upon an average, there will be about three drug-stores to every four blocks! In the country towns, the same fact prevails, in proportion. We know of a small village, a little way out of New York, where an acquaintance of ours eked out a scanty living as the proprietor of a country newspaper, until the thought struck him of setting up a shop for the sale of patent medicines, and drugs generally. There he advertised in his paper, and so great was his custom, that he made quite a handsome little fortune in a few years. It is also notorious that some of the most successful speculations entered into in America are the medicine speculations—mixtures got up by some person, with greater or less degree of knowledge, and, by dint of advertising and keen business talent, sold off in enormous quantities.

These are but partial specimens of the great medicine trade— drops in the ocean. For it is quite oceanic—this dosing, and drugging, and physicing of the great American people!

Does every body, then, take medicine? Is it a regular thing with all classes, rich and poor, old and young? Perhaps not quite so bad as that; and yet the cases of those who do not take medicines of some kind or other, frequently during their lives, are very rare. With many it begins in early childhood and continues through life. Is it not probable that this has much to do with the deficient state of the health, vigor, digestion, and manly physique of America?

We are clear in our own mind that, in by far the vast majority of cases, these medicines do a great deal more hurt than good— that, indeed, they often lay the foundation for a permanent derangement of health, destroy comfort, and shorten life. These are severe words, but we believe them fully warranted by the facts.

It is too generally supposed, (for that is the amount of it) that there is some magic or charm in a mysterious drug, a little vegetable or mineral compound whose nature we do not happen to know, that is going to do the wondrous work of restoring the functions of the body, when disordered, into perfect order and harmony again! And not only this, but all the diversities of age, temperament, combination, degree, etc., are overlooked, and the same drug is supposed capable of curing all the various cases under the same heading!

For there are as many varieties of disease as there are persons diseased; there are hardly any two cases alike, and cannot be. Because the degree and exact state of each person's sickness depend on combinations of circumstances that belong to him alone, and that have met together in no other instance but his. This alone makes the arbitrary use of an arbitrary medicine ridiculous. But there are other points equally important.

Really, to state the matter in plain terms, there can be very little, if any, wholesome effect produced upon almost any case of disease, (probably not one in twenty) from the mere taking of some more or less powerful drug into the stomach, to have whatever effect it may produce upon the bowels, blood, nerves, brain, etc. The more powerful it is, the worse it is. A shock is produced, and perhaps an accelerated action—always to be paid for by a reaction, according to an eternal law of nature. We are not now speaking of marked contingencies, accidents, fits, etc., where prompt and decided means are to be adopted, and where the physician's object is to relieve the patient at once, and let the future make up for any temporary damage he may be compelled to do by those decided means, whatever they are. Our remarks, of course, have no bearing upon such cases as those: but upon the patient and sustained cure of a man laboring under some illness, the result of probably many and long-continued violations of natural laws, and of the simplest requirements of bodily condition. In such cases, (and they make up by far the main portion of the sickness of the civilized world) it is quite certain to our mind, that any reliance upon drugs is futile. The cure must be by other means, and nature, as in all else, is to be looked to, studied, followed, and faithfully relied upon. In general terms it may be stated that the cure must be as slow as the disease was in forming.

SEXUALITY

There is, of course, very much to be said relating to health and strength with reference to habits of sexuality, etc. It ought to be more generally understood that here concentrate what are, in many cases, the most important bearings upon manly soundness, physique, and long life.

Modern habits, in their bearings upon this particular, in all our great cities, may be concealed as far as any allusion to them in print and public discourse is concerned, but they are well known enough for our remarks to be understood and appreciated.

Through the cities, (and we don't know that we need to make an exception of country places either) boys commence early, not only in their knowledge of licentious pleasures, but in their participation of them —increasing rapidly as they advance toward young manhood, and when they take their place in society as full grown members of it, generally with habits formed that, by their effects, stick to them through life. An appearance of decorum is preserved to the outer world; "modesty" is not shocked in parlors or in the social assemblage by any unpleasant word or allusion, but the facts of life, could they be exposed, would be such as to astound the whole mass, even the bad themselves.

If an investigation were candidly made, for that purpose, it would probably be found out that, through the thousands and thousands of different working-men, mechanics, employees, clerks, nearly grown apprentices, etc., in New York, and our other great cities, an immense proportion of them, probably a large majority, have had more or less unfortunate experience with syphilitic disease! This is an appalling fact; yet we are obliged to say we have no doubt it is a fact.

The places of resort for the classes of men and youths just mentioned are, of late years, where licentious habits are advanced and confirmed. We are no moralist, in the usual acceptation of the term, but consider this subject solely in its reference to health and physique. And we must candidly inform the reader, especially the youth, that there is no more deadly foe to manly development than the infusion of the virus of any form of venereal disease, however moderate it may be, through his blood and system. It may remain lurking and lurking there for years, and appear a long while afterward, in terrible forms.

Under the present state of things, among the young and middle aged men, it is a bitter fact that it is not considered anything alarming to be "diseased." You meet that everywhere, and its commonness takes off the edge of its hideousness. But it is really one of the most serious things that can happen to the body, especially in early life. Some of the best physicians assert that after once becoming ingrained in the blood, the syphilitic taint is never afterwards thoroughly worked out of the system. They say it is analogous to the vaccinating matter for vareoloid (a mild form of smallpox affecting people who have already had the disease or have been vaccinated against it); if once the smallest particle "takes," it remains in the body ever afterward.

Writers and speakers are surely too fearful of a little candid speaking upon this subject. It is considered well enough between two persons, or in a small assemblage, but indelicate where a writer is addressing a multitude. We think differently. We believe that ignorance upon this subject is greatly the cause of the evil in the existing state of things; the common classes of young men do not appreciate the fearful detriment they are doing to their manly condition, vigor, and health. Neither are the facts of life, as carried on nightly in the cities, half as well understood by the public as they should be.

Upon this part of the subject we have to add that one of the greatest benefits of training, exercise, simple food, early hours, etc., is that, under them, the sexual passions are far less morbid than under a stimulated course of life. The thoughts are, by degrees, diverted from that form of pleasure, and a tone of greater coolness and evenness pervades the temper. The almost unnatural indulgence in licentiousness, of the desire for it, which previously, perhaps, characterized the man, sinks away, and a different, more wholesome and more salutary habit of feeling and practice succeeds.

BEAUTY

What is beauty? The question is a puzzling one, and has been so in all ages. Much has been written upon it, and, like pleasure, it is supposed to vary among the different races and temperaments. Voltaire says: Ask a Negro of Guinea what is beautiful, and he will answer, that to him it is a black oily skin, sunken eyes, and a flat nose. The devil, (says the same author) if you were to ask him, might tell you that the beautiful consists in a pair of horns, four claws, and a tail; while, if you consult the philosophers, they will answer you with their jargon. We give this because we would like to let our readers see what the great authors have been writing on a subject that all can realize in their own perceptions and sympathies, but that will hardly bear writing about. As for us and our purposes, we would simply impress the fact, (without mixing ourselves up in any argument, or trying to explain reasons why) that, as regards human beings, in an important sense, Beauty is simply health and a sound physique. We can hardly conceive of a man, at any age of life, who is in perfect health, and keeps his person clean and neatly attired, who has not some claims to this much-prized attribute. This may be a new doctrine to many of our readers, but the more it is examined, the more depth it will exhibit.

On the other hand, it is all in vain to pretend that there is any real beauty, or ever can be, in a feeble or deficient man. There is a class of writers, both in this country and Great Britain, who seem to be doing their best, in their novels, sketches, poems, etc., to present as the models for imitation and approval, a set of sickly milk-and-water men, young, middle-aged, or old, without any timber in them, very sentimental, and generally very unwell anyhow. We hope the young fellows who read our remarks will be on their guard against these writers and their sickly models. They are not for live, robust American men—and especially not for our youth. A very different pattern indeed is wanted to be placed before the growing generations.

The ideas of beauty allowed to prevail and take the lead are too much under the control of such sketch-writers, and of the standard of tailors and milliners, fashion-plates, and the like. A pretty, sickly, chalk-and-pink face, either in man or woman, is not beauty. On the contrary, it should be classed with deformed things. Always, in a man, indeed, a certain dash of ugliness, rudeness, and want of prettiness, is found to set off his personal qualities—if he have otherwise perfect health.

71

THE SENSES

Of course, all the senses become healthier, longer lasting in keenness, and more perfect, from the clean and buoyant state of the body which results from continued training. The eyes and sight may be mentioned as likely to be vastly improved, if they were previously ailing. Much of the bad eyesight that we notice is simply from the fact that the whole system wants renovation, the blood being bad, from all sorts of unwholesome and injurious habits. Under good training, continued year after year, the eyes will be likely to continue good through life, however advanced it may prove.

The senses of taste and smell, also; these become dulled from all those luxurious and unwholesome habits we have cautioned the reader against, and that deteriorate the physique and manly perfection. Relieved of their evil influence, the palate and the nostrils remain clear and sound as long as the frame holds together.

Indeed, all the senses, all the functions and attributes of the body, become altogether renewed, more refined, more capable of conferring pleasure in themselves, with far more delicate susceptibilities, under the condition produced by long and faithful observance of good diet, proper exercise, and the other rules of healthy development.

THE FEET

If a man wants personal ease, and even for health we consider it requisite too, he must pay more than the usual attention to the feet, and what is worn upon them. Besides, a great portion of the exercise necessary for health and digestion requires a far better condition of the feet than is common. Probably, in civilized life, half the men have more or less deformed feet, from the tight and wretchedly made boots generally worn.

In one of the feet there are thirty-six bones, and the same number of joints, continually playing in locomotion, and needing always a free and loose action. Yet they are not always squeezed into boots not modeled from them, nor allowing the play and ease do they require. For the modern boot is formed on a dandified idea of beauty, as it is understood at Paris and London, and not as it is exemplified by nature.

If you want to see the feet in their natural and beautiful proportions, you must get a view of the casts of the remains of ancient sculpture, representing the human form, doubtless from the best specimens afforded by the public games and training exercises of the Greek and Roman arenas. They exhibit what the foot is when allowed to grow up, with its free, un-cramped, un-deformed action. There have been no artificial coverings or compressions; and we know that the gait therefrom must have been firm and elastic. We can understand how the Macedonian phalanx, or the Roman legion, performed its long day's march. We can see the ten thousand Greeks pursuing their daily wearying course through the destroying climate of Asia, marching firmly, manfully, across the arid sand, the mountain pass, or the flinty plain. It is a truthful lesson we may learn, not for the soldier only, but for the civilian.

Probably there is no way to have good and easy boots or shoes, except to have lasts modeled exactly to the shape of the feet. This is well worth doing. Hundreds of times the cost of it are yearly spent in idle gratifications—while this, rightly looked upon, is indispensable to comfort and health.

The feet, too, must be kept well-clothed with thin socks in summer, and woolen in winter—and washed daily. We may mention that one of the best remedies for cold feet which many people are troubled with in the winter, is bathing them frequently in cold water. If this does not succeed, add a little exercise.

Too many young men, and other men too, seriously injure their health by carelessly going with poorly protected feet, or even with improperly made boots. These last, from the distress they cause by walking, indispose to exercise—which would very likely be otherwise engaged in with eagerness and pleasure. It is also to be noted, that one who makes a regular practice to bathe his feet daily, wear clean socks, and protect himself during bad weather by good boots or shoes, will hardly stop there—but will, ten chances to one, continue on until he habitually observes all the rules necessary to a clean and robust development.

CHAPTER 8

PRIZE FIGHTING

CONSIDERING THE IMMENSE prejudices of those who give the cue, we do not so much wonder at the aversion which most of the intellectual and benevolent members of the community feel toward Prize Fighting as an "institution," and which has been called forth quite loudly and generally by the late contest between Morrissey and Heenan. At first thought, perhaps, it seems a savage and unchristian performance, for two men to go deliberately to work, to pound and batter each other, merely for the purpose of seeing who can stand the most "punishment," and do the greatest credit to his muscle, game and training. Yet (we would suggest to the reader), the question is not so abruptly decided. There are other considerations and arguments—some of them quite important. It appears, of late, as if all the indignation which might justifiably be directed towards the sins of different departments of modern life, theological, political, social, etc., were withdrawn from the rest, and turned towards the performances of the prize ring, and of those who "go in" for that amusement and branch of "science."

The vast under stratum of the people, however, will continue to gratify their tastes and impulses, irrespective of the tone of polished society (so called). And it is useless to deny that, through the great masses of men who form that under-stratum, there is a deathless interest in these contests for physical superiority, whether expressed in a battle between two ships-of-war upon the sea, or opposing armies upon land—or, on a smaller scale, between two trained specimens of humanity in the prize ring. There is, we may also say in passing, not an argument against the combat of the prize fight, that does not equally apply to war—to all war, at least, except that for the purpose of resisting the invasion of a foreign foe.

For our own part, we believe in the necessity of those means that help to develop a hardy, robust and combative nation, and desire to see America in that list. We do not think that community able to take care of its rights, and defend them successfully against all odds, where there exist only peaceful, pious, respectable and orthodox citizens. There must be something more. What, for instance, did ancient Rome rise out of? How came she to be the commanding power of the world for so many centuries—the leader and master of all lands? Of course, from a plentiful infusion of just about such temper and audacity as congregated at Long Point, around the ropes that enclosed Morrissey and Heenan, the other day. And the subject nations which Rome conquered, one after another, in all directions, were conquered, in many signal cases, because they disdained the fierce encouragements to produce a race of men who could and would fight, not by rote merely, but for the love of fight.

Do we then, (perhaps the amazed reader asks) openly countenance the training of men for prize-fighting? We answer, explicitly, we do, (of course, no one but the writer of these sketches being responsible or implicated in the opinion—it being uttered for himself alone.) It is about time to meet the floods of mawkish milk and water that are poured out upon the land, and which, if justified and put in practice, would crowd America with nothing but puny and feeble men, obedient, pious—a race, half, or perhaps wholly emasculated.

There is, of late years, an excess of philanthropy, which o'er leaps itself, and falls on the other side. We believe it would be a first-rate thing in New York, and all the other cities of the United States, if the science of fighting were made a regular branch of a young man's education—and if the exhibition of contests for physical superiority were common. Some such thing appears to be necessary, to meet the morbid weakness we have alluded to; it is, indeed, with other causes, deteriorating the race, we sometimes think. It appears to have taken possession of almost all the literary classes, and of the preachers and lecturers.

Nor are we afraid of the Americans being too combative. That is a matter which will regulate itself. There are too many varieties and competitors, North, South, East and West—and the mutual attrition of each is beneficial to all the rest. This serves to keep each individual part of it in its due place and proportion, without

75

danger of successful aggression upon the others. But especially in the commercial and older settled states, we are free to confess we are sadly in fear of the danger of seeing that "love of fight" we have alluded to, almost extinguished.

Some such suggestions as these, at least, are certainly called for to counterbalance the tone of writing and expression which lately prevails in select society, with reference to the principle of physical combats for superiority—as if there were not something inspiriting and honorable in such a contest, as in others which involve different leading talents and powers of humanity. Is there not even a high order of heroism in the willingness and capacity to endure the most terrible blows of an opponent, and stand up under them as long as the sinews of the body answer the volition of the mind? Let others say what they will, we say there is—and we say, moreover, that it is a kind of heroism which we need more of in these latitudes—or rather we need the recognition of it—for we do not doubt there is plenty of the quality itself among the common people.

No amount of cultivation, intellect, or wealth, will ever make up to a community for the lack of manly muscle, ability and pluck. History is full of examples of intellectually developed nations, but intellectual only, falling a prey to others of inferior mental calibre, but of daring and overwhelming physique. Even Rome itself, in time, for such reasons, fell a prey to outside invaders far inferior to itself.

We will now proceed to draw a few inferences from the Morrissey and Heenan fight itself:

Probably the best moral to be deduced from the late fight is, that the quality of being able to endure any quantity of blows and bruises, and hold out toughly under them, is what most tells, and gives the final account of itself in a fight. This is what won the victory; while, on the other hand, we should say that, beyond question, no man who has seen only twenty-two or three years, (Heenan's age) is really fit for the grandest exhibition of his bodily powers. The common opinion that about that period of life affords the best show of strength and endurance, under favorable circumstances, is unquestionably an error, and a very great one. Five or six years more are required to give the human frame its

76

settled strength and knit—and the friends of Heenan ought to know this fact, and inculcate it in his mind, t o o . If he wishes to hold out in the result, (not the beginning, mind, but the result!) he must avoid overtaxing his powers too soon. The hard oaken fiber of the frame does not come at his years—or during the earliest years anyhow.

The fight itself is, perhaps, the best illustration of what we say here, and often have said. How splendidly Heenan began it! There was, perhaps, never seen a finer show of determination, brawn, and alertness than that much-talked-of "first round," and Heenan's part in it—giving his friends undreamed-of hope, and equally discouraging to those of the opposite faction. It seemed as if there was no standing against those quick and terrible blows. But there was; and that made the very fact which was to bear away the palm from him who commenced so well. He began well, but could not hold out to the last in proportion; that spoilt all, and must ever spoil all.

The rule holds true in more cases than this of the prize fight. It runs through all that is to be said upon the subject of physical training for a man's health and vigor, and involves its most important bearings. We say, therefore, that the late fight bears a great lesson in the fierce attacks and defenses of its rapid twenty-two minutes—the lesson that he wins who can "best stand grief," as the sporting fraternity quaintly phrase it.

Or, in other words, in robust training for this life, which is it-self a continual fight with some form of adversary or other, the aim should be to form that solid and adamantine fire which will endure long and serious attacks upon it, and come out unharmed from them, rather than

the ability to perform sudden and brilliant feats, which often exhaust the powers in show, without doing any substantial good. We know nothing of John Morrissey, but consider ourselves obliged to him, and his theory and tactics of fighting, for a marked example of this main element of our hints upon the general physical training of American young men.

It is for such reasons, among the rest, that we dwell upon this fight—an illustration, as it is, of such practical details of diet, exercise, abstinence, etc., as our foregoing papers would suggest for

77

general use, as far as may be—because, of course, the actual necessity of this kind of training, for fighting purposes, will never be the rule, but only the exception. Still it is to be admitted that nothing short of a prize-fight will ever bring the rules of manly health and training to that system- atic perfection which they are attaining, and out of which we, among the rest, have been able to write these articles for popular use.

Just in the way as the institution of the horse-race, and nothing less than that, brings the breed of the horse up to a far, very far, higher pitch of physical perfection than could be attained by any other means known or possible upon earth—just exactly in the same way, (after all the talk, pro and con, has been expended about it) it remains to be distinctly confessed that nothing short of these fierce manly contests, in ancient and modern times, has led to the mightiest and most perfect development of the masculine frame, and proved what are the real rules consonant with its soundest physiology.

Therefore, in opposition to the views expressed by the editors of the American newspapers, (the Atlas, we believe, among the rest) we say a stern word or two, not in defense of these fights only, but in deliberate advocacy of them. We are writing just as fast as our pen can gallop over the paper—no doubt skip many of the points we should like to make, on our side of the arguments, if we had time to stop and arrange the said arguments in imposing array. At present we only throw out our views, as the Tartar shoots his arrow, passing along at full speed. But in some way, on some future occasion, we intend to resume this subject, and present our views with more preparation and effect.

By the way, the same papers that have such indignant editorials about the fight are the very ones in which we have noticed, of late, quite a good many articles bewailing the physical degeneracy of the race of men in America—statements that we are getting to have, in our cities, and on all sides, too many inferior and feeble men. Why, it is for the very reason, among the rest, that the tone of those who assume to lead in public education, public opinion, the press, etc., sounds continually in the key it does, that there is indeed too much of this same degeneracy. As we have before remarked in these off-hand sketches, the spirit of American schools, authors, etc., tends to continually develop the intellect and refinement of taste of the people, at the expense of all their bodily stoutness, muscle, and their indifference to little elegancies, niceties, and parlor and college models. We would have this met and reversed. Not that we have any objection to the colleges and the parlors—they are, of course, well enough; but they do not afford that broad and earth-deep under-stratum that is necessary for a nation with a resistless physique. Something a little more coarse and rank is necessary. Let the tone of public taste, instead of refusing any connivance with the vast undertow of popular sympathy with these muscular combats, and all that appertains to them, be turned to elevate and improve the said combats, and make them, it may be, far better than they are, retaining, however, the same fierce energy and combative science. We are not afraid to say, once again, that at this present writing, we are decidedly in favor of some such course as this.

As to the point of physical degeneracy here in the United States, we do not, upon the whole, make much account of it. The nation is passing through several important physiological processes and combinations. To a great degree, it is yet getting acclimated—especially in the West, and on the Pacific coast, which latter is destined to have a huge influence on the future physique of America. In its dry, wholesome, life-giving and life-preserving atmosphere, the human form, it may be, is destined to attain its grandest proportions, clearness, and longevity. We allude to California and Oregon, and indeed the immense inland stretch from Kansas down through Utah and Arizona, to the borders of Mexico. Here the air is dry and antiseptic—everything grows to a size, strength and expanse, unknown in the Northern and Eastern States. Nature is on a large scale; and here, in time to come, will be found a wonderful race of men.

Before dismissing the subject of the late fight, we would once more specially call the attention of the reader to the astonishing power of the trained human body to endure and make light of, those indescribably strong and bloody attacks, blows, and bruises, which would be certain death to half a dozen men such as we usually see walking the streets of New York and Brooklyn. What a marvelous power this is, which enables the human body to pass off, as if in sport, such a fearful battering and pounding. We may, we say, learn a valuable lesson here, and apply it to the warding off of disease, and in the usages of everyday life.

In the same train of thought, we would remark that the "sporting men" of our American cities afford quite a study, in connection with the subject of manly training. There are among them some of the finest specimens of physique, in the world. Indeed, generally they are a handsome race of men. You will see among them a number who are quite advanced in years, yet in a good state of preservation. They are generally distinguished by a certain smartness in their attire, quick movements, and by a bold, sharp, and determined expression of the countenance.

It is astonishing how much "fast life" many of these fellows go through, and come out quite unharmed. Often, we have thought, they set at defiance the ordinary rules of health and medicine, and baffle what are supposed to be the surest canons of the laws of longevity— coming out quite unscathed, and going on their ordinary course, hearty and good-looking, as if nothing had happened. But it is to be noticed, at the same time, that such specimens are of callous temper- ament, reckless, without any of the attributes of the finer feelings, and not disposed to stand about trifles, either of conscience or anything else.

We have sometimes even thought, while standing among a large crowd of these sporting men, in some Broadway drinking saloon, or some such place, and quietly observing their actions and looks that they presented about the best collection of specimens of hardy and developed physique we had anywhere seen. Their movements remind one of a fine animal. They have that clear, audacious, self-confident expression of the eye, and of the face generally, which marks some of the animals in a wild state. Notice the attitudes of them as they stand, or lean; the extended arm holding the glass of liquor, and raising it to the lips; the hat tipped down in front over the eyebrow; the "Gallus" style generally. Or, see two of them square off at each other in a joking way; the limber vibration of the upper part of the body upon the waist; one foot planted forward; the movements of the arms, and the poise of the neck.

So much for the "sporting men," for they afford us a study, with the rest. And, indeed, in casting our eyes around, we feel disposed to take all the "muscle," indiscriminately, under our favor, and speak a good word for it—to counterbalance the disfavor which is so generally shown toward it.

Of course the young reader, or any reader, will have sense enough to understand that we do not pick out the life of a "sport" from all the rest, and offer it to him as a pure model for him to follow, to the rejection of the others. We express no opinion, and give no advice about it. We simply call attention to the singularly perfect physique of these men, in contradistinction to those shambling professional and genteel persons, clerks, lawyers, pious students, correct youths and middle-aged men, and the life—pale, feeble, timid, quiet, dyspeptic, and uninteresting generally, either for the company of man or woman. And as to real viciousness, let no one suppose that it is confined to any one class of the community, or is any more to be found in those who "lead a gay life," than in those who keep demure faces, and are supposed to be lawful and orthodox—that is to say, the latter, in most cases, add hypocrisy to the natural sins of man, and to the private indulgence in the same.

CHAPTER 9

CLIMATE

MUCH IS SAID, (and with reason) on the advantages of climate. The principal points of climate, in the line of latitude of New York, New England, and the Middle States, from which injury ensues to the best physical requisites of our common humanity, arise from the vast differences of temperature between a great part of the winter weather—and a great part of the summer weather —the one being often extremely hot, and the other extremely cold. Also, the sudden changes and fluctuations to which we hereabouts are liable—the same week occasionally presenting nearly all the varieties of temperature from those of the arctic regions to those on the line of the equator.

It is often argued that the human frame and organization cannot be expected to stand these amazing discords and shocks of temperature, and that it will not; consequently, if such premises be true, that a hardy, sound, large-bodied and long-lived race of men cannot flourish in such a climate—cannot stand it, for the course of permanent generations. The assertion is plausible—and yet it will not bear to be thoroughly investigated. Climate has much, very much, to do with the physique, as with all else that appertains to a nation, (its literature, laws, religion, manners, etc.); but so marvellously can the human being adapt himself to circumstances that there is hardly any climate on the surface of the globe, but, as far as it alone is concerned, can be made to adjust itself to manly development and fine condition.

Indeed it seems as if some of the most rugged and unfavorable climates turn out the noblest specimens of men—as, in Europe, from Scandinavia descended the very best parts of the elements, which served to make that composite, the English race—flowing onward to be but an element of a greater and stronger composite race still, namely, the American. From that Northern Europe, and from chilly and sterile Germania, we inherit, doubtless, we say, the toughest and most commanding part of our physique; leaving for sunnier climes to have bequeathed us what are perhaps our finer mental and sentimental attitudes. (And yet there are not a few who will contend that for the latter qualities also, the best of them, we owe, far, far back in the past, the debt of obligation to our Teutonic ancestors, many hundreds, perhaps thousands of years ago.)

In those bleak and changeable climes, too, men lived to a great age, and performed heroic deeds—no parlor gentlemen, but such as held their own in the violent combats of the open air, and upon the sea. A new age is upon us—and yet the same old qualities, and the love and admiration of them, still remain. These qualities are to exist and find their expression in new forms, conformable to modern life, usages, and tastes. Otherwise, we shall have but a nation of smirking persons, polite, dapper, genteel and correct, following the established forms, their shrunken frames concealed in costumes, because, if they were stripped, their meagreness and deformity would disgust the world. Indeed, it has sometimes appeared as if the hardiest races must necessarily flourish in rugged and stern climates; for that, among the rest, awakes them to exertion, labor, knowledge, and ingenuity, which develop the great qualities of a man. A perfect man is the result of urged cultivation. Nothing brings him out either so much as "a forced put." He then enters into that combat with Nature, and with circumstances, which hardens his powers, teaches him his own grandeur, and begets in him the fierce joy of combativeness and conquest.

The physique, of course, partakes largely of all this place of causes and effects. It soon learns to confront the evils that to a feeble person are so terrible—learns to find some of its highest pleasures in overcoming them. Thus, storms, the cold, exposure, the sea, perils, enemies, war—all these, and the like of these, to superior and hardier spirits, instead of giving terror, give a certain sort of grim and manly delight. They are the atmosphere most suitable to them—the aliment which suits them. A little examination, then, may perhaps show that the really superb physique of man, involving his greatest heroism, faith, and unconquerable spirit of freedom, owes its birth and breed, not to the genial climes of this earth of ours, where the air is soft and equable, and fruits and perfumes run their even round the whole year, and where man has no effort to make for the support of his existence, but is permitted to lounge an indolent holiday of life, and dream it away in the poetic enjoyments of his appetites and amours,—but to rougher and sturdier lands, where he has to fight hand-to-hand with the very earth, air, and sea. Thus truly, Mother Earth, whose sharpness is only sweetness in disguise, raises her firmer races. Ever, she seems to show, through the affairs of man, that he must be whipped and spurred into his best development. By that means, and nothing less, will he arrive at all the highest prizes and blessings of his life.

From such trains of thought and argument, we arrive at the conclusion that, allowing all which is charged against the climate of the northern portions of the United States, (and including Canada) there is nothing to prevent our seeing there the very grandest examples of physique, strength, quickness, tone, and longevity—and these, for permanent continuance, through many an age and generation of the future. But in order to produce these effects, the public mind needs far more clearly to understand, (and act thoroughly and persistently on the understanding) that certain means are indispensable, for individuals, that they may resist the injurious wear and tear of a racking and variable climate. A man must become, as we intimated in the beginning of our articles, a reasoning and reasonable being—must be willing to follow a certain course, and find his pay for the same, not in ephemeral and immediate gratifications, but those at some distance; must be willing to place health, sound internal organs, and perfect condition, at the head of the list of the objects of his whole life, here on earth.

The cold bath, for instance, cautiously begun, and kept up habitually morning after morning, year after year—what a toughener and hardener to this changeable climate of ours it is! In conjunction with other means, (for, be it remembered, the true theory of health is not a "one idea" theory, but involves a cluster, all hanging together) it neutralizes the differences of the air, different weeks and seasons, and makes the body indifferent to them—thriving equally under the heats of August or in the bitter contracting air of January or December.

This simple habit, (which would occupy from five to ten minutes of your before-breakfast time) is enough to ensure the frame, in by far the greatest number of cases, from the common and prevalent injury of colds, coughs, etc.

The modern custom of heating by stoves has much to do with the incompatibility of a large proportion of our North Americans, with the climate in which they live. Given close rooms, hot stoves and no ventilation, and you have a prolific crop of chilled bodies, whenever exposed to the otherwise bracing effects of the open air. It does not seem to be known that the best way to keep really warm in winter, (for men) is, not to withdraw from the open air, but go out in it, and keep stirring. Habit soon settles the matter. Fifty and sixty years ago, before the introduction of cast-iron stoves, there was far more hardy-hood of body, and less liability to coughs, and all forms of pulmonary complaints.

Indeed, upon deliberate reflection, it would be found that many, perhaps most, of the evils which are laid to the American climate, in the northern and eastern states, are not so much to be attributed to it, as to special causes—the habits of life, the follies of dress, unwise diet, artificial overheating, and the like. This leads us to consider a special point; in the matter of diet, which, although touched upon incidentally in our foregoing articles, is of importance enough to call for its own heading.

MEAT AS THE PRINCIPAL DIET FOR THE INHABITANTS OF THE NORTHERN STATES.

In our view, if nine-tenths of all the various culinary preparations and combinations, vegetables, pastry, soups, stews, sweets, baked dishes, salads, things fried in grease, and all the vast array of confections, creams, pies, jellies, etc., were utterly swept aside from the habitual eating of the people, and a simple meat diet substituted in their place—we will be candid about it, and say in plain words, an almost exclusive meat diet—the result would be greatly, very greatly, in favor of that noble-bodied, pure-blooded, and superior race we have had a leaning toward, in these articles of ours. The effect of nearly all of these highly artificial dishes is to stimulate and goad on the appetite, distend the stomach, thin the blood, and prepare the way for some form or other of disease. They do not harden a man in his fibre, nor make him any the better in wholesome flesh—as it is often to be noticed of such articles that the greatest eaters of them are by no means the fattest, but often lean and scraggly.

The business of eating, in modern civilized life, is probably conducted on the most marked absence of principles, or of anything like reason or science, of aught that can be mentioned. And yet there is nothing in which there may be and ought to be more science displayed. It is here where physiology and medicine have yet to make their great foundational beginnings—for with all the cry about medical accomplishment, in our times, it is plainly to be seen that, as far as the masses of the people are concerned, there is the same state of ignorance and darkness prevalent, that can be shown as marking any of the ages of the past.

We have been flooded in America, during the last fifteen or twenty years, with vast numbers of doctors, books, theories, publications, etc., whose general drift, with respect to diet, had been to make people live altogether on dry bread, stewed apples, or similar interesting stuff. What volumes of works have been issued from the different publishing houses, of which the foregoing is about the amount! Probably a more monstrous and enfeebling school could not be started; and yet it has undoubtedly obtained considerable foothold in the United States, especially in New England. In the latter quarter, the people are prone to be too intellectual, and to be "ashamed of the carnal body"—running very much to brains, at the expense of the brawn and muscle of their limbs. It is for this reason probably that in the eastern states the school we allude to have met with the greatest favor, and number the main part of their followers.

But in defiance of all that can be said in behalf of dry bread and stewed apples (good enough diet to deplete the system, at times, or in case of a fit of half sickness) we have no hesitation in publicly declaring our adherence to the motto previously inscribed—Let the main part of the diet be meat, to the exclusion of all else. The result of this would be that the digestive organs would have more than half the labor (agonizing labor, it often is) withdrawn from them, and the blood relieved from an equally great amount of noxious deposit which, under the present system, is thrown into it.

This is very likely an astounding doctrine to the reader, who has perhaps been taught to believe under the teachings of the school afore, that "temperance in eating" means vegetarianism, with all its weakening effects. But ours is the true doctrine, in our judgment, for all the northern and eastern states. We say less about hotter climates, because in those regions of perpetual fruits, there are other points to be considered. And it may be as well to add, that by meat diet, we do not mean the eating of meat cooked in grease and saturated therewith—or in any made dishes—but meat simply cooked, broiled, roasted, or the like. This is the natural eating of man and woman, under the first and unbiased appetites, and confirmed afterwards by the experience and the researches of reason.

"LOATHED MELANCHOLY"

INDIVIDUAL AND NATIONAL

AND THE ONLY RADICAL CURE

Brooding and all sorts of acrid thoughts, "the blues," and the varied train of depressed feelings, are among the most serious enemies of a fine physique—while the latter, in turn, possesses a marvellous power of scattering all those unpleasant visitors, and dissipating them to the winds. It is at least probable, we begin by saying, that in a vast majority of cases, melancholy of mind is the exclusive result of a disordered state of the body—a longer or shorter absence of those clarifying habits of diet, exercise, etc., which we have in previous articles jotted down for observance. If the victim of "the horrors" could but pluck up energy enough, after turning the key of his door-lock, to strip off all his clothes and give his whole body a stinging rub-down with a flesh-brush till the skin becomes all red and aglow—then, donning his clothes again, take a long and brisk walk in the open air, expanding the chest and inhaling plentiful supplies of the health-giving element—ten to one but he would be thoroughly cured of his depression, by this alone. Such habits, and what corresponds with them, becoming common, and especially if backed up with regular employment occupying the mind and the bodily powers for a stated portion of the day, and it were probable that the most inveterate case of melancholy would yield to those simple and harmless prescriptions.

For it is not generally realized what a wide circle of victims there is to this "ennui"—this word of France we have imported, for the English tongue hardly has any fit phrase to describe it. If one were to set out investigating the matter, it would probably be found that these victims exist in almost countless numbers, in all ranks of people in America, the working classes just the same as the rich Not only the idler in his parlor, and without any need of occupying his time in an employment to procure his living—not only the literary man, with his overstrained mentality—or the professional person, the lawyer at his desk, the clergyman in his study, the student at his books—not these any more than the mechanic, the farmer, the carpenter, mason, boatman—and especially those of sedentary employments, the printer, shoemaker, tailor, and others at their listless work indoors—all, all are to be numbered among the habitual sufferers from the cause we have mentioned. Nor would our hints be complete without some allusion to this one of the most serious detriments to all the wholesome operations of the manly system, sapping the strength and shortening life.

What does this too prevailing melancholy in such people result from? From their bad condition of body, very generally—the reaction of the powers, often from the stimulus of drink, or other exciting causes. In those that do not drink, the stomach and nervous system are very likely out of order, after months, perhaps years, of heedless violations of natural laws—a long curse of artificial living, depositing its bad dregs at last in such a way that they have effectually clogged that natural buoyancy and lightness of temperament, that nonchalance and even gaiety, which seem to be at least as much the birthright of man as of any other animal. A sad and terri- ble price, is it not, at which even civilization and the splendid results of these improvements of arts, literature, laws, and social culture, may almost be considered to cost too much? For this same curse of sadness, in its numberless forms, is an attribute of civilized life, and must be met with those weapons which can destroy it—an infusion through civilized life of a greater degree of natural physical habits, and a stern rejection of those specious enjoyments that leave such frightful deposits afterward, that sting and fester through the middle and later years.

Nor let anyone be deceived in this matter of low spirits, by the outside appearance of people as they move about in the streets, in public houses, places of amusement, etc. In public, no doubt you would judge from the show upon the surface that everyone was happy, and that there was no such thing as a cloud upon the sky of the mind; all goes so well, and there is so much drinking and eating, and joking and laughing and gay music. The faces are full of color, the eyes sparkle, the voices have a ring—everybody is well dressed, and there is surely no unhappiness in these lives. A serious mistake! Many and many a silent hour, both by day and night, does everyone here undergo, in which the distress of the mind equals any distress of the body, in its worst sickness or hurt. The evil we speak of, like most other human evils, is not of a kind that flaunts out and exposes itself, but is only to be detected by the powers of insight and acute observation. To those powers there is perhaps no rank of the community, and no group of men collected together, but the presence of it can be plainly seen, passive enough, but still lurking there. It shows itself in the lines of the face, cut and seamed by harassing thoughts, and many an hour of discontent and nausea of life. The very classes that would be supposed to be freest from the visitations of this grim spir- it—those who live a gay and reckless life, following where the animal passions lead and the appetite of gain—even those whose career is the career of prostitution, "pleasure" and play—are the very persons who give some of the most striking illustrations of its presence and effects. Some of the members of these classes (we were going to say all of them) are subject to terrible fits of despondency and "the horrors," lasting day after day, and even, in a few instances, for weeks on the stretch—a curious study for those inquirers who indeed think that the proper study for mankind is man, with all the strange play of his interwoven warp of passions, appetites, pains and joys.

Further than this, the middle ranks of society, the sturdy body of American workingmen, even the young; afford plentiful examples of a similar sort. There seems to be something, not only in our Saxon stock, but in all the inter-grafts we have here in America from the Celtic nations also, that forms the popular disposition, at times, to fits of melancholy—each individual after his or her own form special of outlet and expression. Otherwise we should be unable to account for the fact of so many of the class we have mentioned being included in the list. For that they are included we feel certain. What one of them but has his periods, (in a majority of cases frequent, and in many severe) sombre and gloomy fits, when the whole world appears cheerless and bleak, and the best of life not worth the living? During these fits, any effort at conversation is unpleasant, and the machinery of the mind turns with a slow motion—no alertness, no spring or vivacity—incapacitated from all the talents and accomplishments that are ready enough at other times. Sometimes, in the working classes, these periods of depression become habitual, and take up the majority of the years of life—more usually in the cases of those whose occupations are sedentary, as in those, before-mentioned, of tailors, shoemakers, etc.

All we are here saying is but the candid mention of a series of pregnant and positive facts, which it is impossible to deny, and which will be readily admitted by those who have looked with thinking eyes through the strata of middle society—not on the surface merely, but down in its recesses, in habits, homes, occupations, and especially during those hours when life is lived according to what itself is, inherently, and not from second-hand influences, imitation, gentility, or disguises, or, "the looks." We know very well that the subject we treat of is not often, hardly ever, indeed, mentioned in this way; but we are clear that it ought to be mentioned, and met, too, as every other great fact of bearings on the popular happiness or unhappiness should be. This is the only way of getting at such things, and it is all folly to cover them up or avoid them.

Through the "upper" ranks of society, it is well known, the under- tone of existence is that of listlessness and low spir- its—running in every vein of fashionable dawdling and occupa- tion. The same cast appears in literature, in every volume where the imagination bears a part, giving a heavy and depressing cast to all. The novel-hero of the writers is always a gentleman who has sentimental moods—also, misfortunes and tragic adventures, placing him in all sorts of forlorn predicaments; and the same with tragedies. But we will not travel aside from our own special track.

We have dwelt at more length on this topic of "the blues," (to give it that expressive and can't name, which is common) because we are firmly convinced that the hint we uttered at the commencement of our remarks on this branch, is possessed of the true secret of pricking and bursting the bubble—for bubble it is, even allowing all that can be said of hereditary tendency. That same tendency not only has the weakness itself, but the strength, reason, and ability to surmount it, under proper circumstances. The observance of the laws of manly training, duly followed, can utterly rout and do away with the curse of a depressed mind, melancholy, "ennui," which now, in more than half the men of America, blights a large portion of the days of their existence. Of this we have not the least particle of doubt—and, indeed, the thing stands to reason.

We repeat it, that it is the bad stuff stagnating in the physical system, accumulated through long seasons of artificial eating, drinking, and "pleasure," (a sad mistake of a name as generally applied) that returns in a morbid action of the mind and temper. This is the true cause at the bottom of that painful and wide-spread effect. We are not sure but the same cause is at the bottom of another still more dreadful effect—Insanity. Such was Spurzheim's deliberate opinion, if we are not mistaken in our inferences from the hints he drops in his work on that terrible malady. This celebrated and keen observer and student, after passing through all that could be found and got at, treating insanity as a "disease of the mind," seems to have learned at last that the most important points lay in another direction—physical facts and causes, including, of course, the hereditary ones. And all brooding and melancholy are the first faint tinges, of which insanity is the set color, deep and strong.

Of this aforesaid varied group of ills, then and therefore, we are firm in the conviction that the point of concentration, where, by medical men, the same as the rest, and perhaps more than the first, they are to be studied, and from which, as originally, they all spring, finally they are all to be touched there for the only effectual cure, is the point of the physical. The body—the stomach—the blood—the nervous system— the physical brain, and what affects it for good or

91

bad—in other words, a rational and elevated system of MANLY TRAINING—we believe that knowledge and practice in that direction only will put to effectual flight all the phantom swarms of "loathed melancholy," so threatening with their growth of worse mental derangements, now prevalent through the many classes of men here in the United States.

Have we made ourselves understood? For it is no small thing, reader, we have taken upon ourselves to treat in this section of our hints, and we have thrown out, in a rapid manner, these suggestions, in all candor, more to open the subject, and lead you to think upon it yourself, and to behold it in what we are sure is its true light, to be deliberated upon thoughtfully afterwards, than as any finished presentation of our views upon it.

There is such a deplorable ignorance everywhere, (we are more and more convinced) of the surpassing importance of these physical considerations—these which refer to the human being, as a perfect animal, and to the sublime science of breeding a nation of sane and clean-fleshed men. All treatment of evils of any sort whatever, especially those evils we have just been considering, that contemplates anything less than such a science, it but patchwork and poor botching. We are, therefore, unable to apply other terms than those which end the last sentence to the usual "reforms" of the theorists of the day—as to most of the schools of the doctors, the meta-physicians, and the moralists, of which America is so rife.

When we hear the preachers preaching from their pulpits, and the lecturers from their platforms—and all the outpourings of the numerous well-intended philanthropists who flood New York with their "May anniversaries," and gatherings at the same—we see clearly enough, for our own satisfaction, that, (putting them all in a bundle together) the wisdom and application of their efforts is just precisely the wisdom of him who should attempt to medicate the superficial sores and boils on a sick body, by nothing better than surface applications, (or by praying to the sores and boils, and exhorting them to be gone!) when the only cure, in the mind of a sensible person worth trial, is the deep, interior, sane cure of the whole quality of the blood and the tissues it forms, which make the body—a generative and altogether physical

cure, involving years of time, and revolution of habits—this the
the vaunted reformers appear never to think of.

CHAPTER 10

VIRILITY

THE NOBLEST FUNCTION of mankind, the power to procreate the soundest and most perfect offspring, ought to remain to a man all through those years we have mentioned in a preceding article, as eligible, under proper training, for him to be in a high, flush condition of health, strength, beauty and happiness—namely, from the twenty-third or fourth to at least the sixty-fifth year of his age. If, during his early years, he become diseased with any form of venereal taint—especially if that be repeated upon him again and again, as in too many cases— of course there is so much strength, and the prospect of longevity taken away; which, in the same train, deprive his system of its true procreative power. A man that exhausts himself continually among women, is not fit to be, and cannot be, the father of sound and manly children. They will be puny and scrofulous—a torment to themselves and to those who have the charge of them.

This virile power, so becoming to a man, and without which, indeed, he is not a man, seems, in modern life, to be under the curse of an insane appetite, especially among the youth of cities, which makes them think they are doing great things if they commence early with women, and keep up afterwards a huge number of intrigues and amours—having no choice about it, but sweeping at all that is female, as a fisherman sweeps fish into his net. This is one reason we see the lamentable spectacle, in New York, and other cities, of so many old-men boys—youths who have begun long before their time, and will never know the true feelings and attributes of that, in some respects, most glorious age, from fourteen years to twenty-one or two—but jump at once from the traits and tastes of childhood, unto all the experiences of mature age. We say this state of things is throwing a bad ingredient in the stock of the population of our cities. You see them in all directions, not without good qualities, perhaps, but in their physique feeble, small, and pale—not the large and rude-natured specimens of humanity that would seem to be called for in America. Their offspring, when in time they marry and have families, illustrate what we said in the first part of our paragraph, and, indeed, if we must be candid about it, are no credit either to their parentage or to the land.

It is related of the ancient Germans, by the Roman writers of that time, that, although in a harsh climate and with a rugged soil, they produced the finest races of men, as far as physique was concerned, then known; and also that it was the stern custom of Germania, in those primitive periods, for the young men to be so educated and trained that they had nothing to do with women till they were twenty six or seven years old. Our readers can ponder a while over these facts, for they are full of meaning.

There is no doubt, as things now are, among the young men of modern civilized life, in cities, that a healthy manly virility seems to be almost lost—seems to have given place to a morbid, almost insane, pursuit of women, especially of the lowest ranges of them, for the mere repetition of the sensual pleasure. This habit, begun by a young fellow, (generally from the contagion of his companions) and afterward formed into a regular indulgence, that is a case where there cannot be produced by training or any other means, a superior specimen of animal perfection, strength and beauty.

We have not read Dr. Sanger's late work, of which so much is said on the subject of female prostitution; but we dare say he has overlooked some of the most important points connected with the subject. For, great as the facts and their bearings are, with reference to the females themselves, the prostitutes, we think the most weighty of the facts, and all their bearings, out of this subject of prostitution, are those which affect men. The effects of prostitution upon men—there is the text for the work that should be written. It involves deep studies and investigations, through the popular strata of modern life—all through the masses of youth, and of men of the younger ranks, (and older ranks, too, for that matter) in the cities,—and then radiating back again into the country regions. To us, in this time, and from the point of view we are now taking it is the question of physique that is affected, and of the race as a fine collection of animals—but out of that, of course, is developed all the rest, the effects upon the minds, morals, social usages, tempers, perpetuity, etc., of the immense rounds of persons further affected by their causes.

One thing is very certain to any man who is at all familiar with the popular under-strata of the life of our great cities—not that mere life upon the surface; a thin glaze of respectability and decorum which, we suppose, deceives only those who either willingly shut their eyes, or have very little power of vision anyhow.

It is, we say, quite certain that, at this very hour, there is circulating through nearly all of the life-streams of this city, and of all great cities, a sure and increasing amount of the tainted blood of prostitution, morbid, venereal and scrofulous—and that there is probably not a street in New York where it does not now exist, and show its effects in human veins, on the human countenance, and in the birth of an enfeebled offspring.

Those are the facts to which we would like to call passing attention, by virtue of our duty as a writer on this subject of health—and considering it, not only in the matter of the daily wholesome observances we have advised, but deeper, as an important race question, and one affected, in a most serious manner, and likely to be affected far more deeply, by the existence of the facts just treated upon.

MUSCULAR POWER & ENDURANCE

We have before intimated that we feel inclined to doubt whether we have, hereabout, any examples of the utmost perfection of muscular power and endurance which man is capable of attaining to. The feats performed by the "strong men" of the shows are worthy of attention, as far as they go; but, when we have inquired into the special cases of the said "strong men," we have invariably found that each individual was the victim of habits which retarded the full development of his power. In all such cases, the power continues as a sort of monstrosity for a year or two, and the "strong man" then becomes perhaps a poor wreck, the ruins of what might have easily lasted through a long life, and been far more highly developed under a proper and sustained course of physical training.

Nothing indeed, amid the infinite wonders of nature, is a

greater wonder than the muscular strength of certain specimens of the human body, even as things are, and have been. Many of these specimens, both in old times and new, are well authenticated. Especially in former days, when physical superiority was more generally   attended to and admired than now, were there marked cases of this immense bodily energy. The relation and perusal of some of them are well calculated to provoke serviceable thoughts in the mind, and to beget a manly emulation in the same course.

In the Greek city of Krotona, in ancient times, one of the athletes, named Milo, accustomed himself from early years, by almost imperceptible degrees, to carry burthens of increasing weight, day after day—joining to that, of course, the other means of producing and confirming the strength and fibre of his body. He persisted in this a number of years, until at last it is credibly reported, that in the height and strength of his vigor, he actually carried an ox four years old, and weighing upwards of a thousand pounds, for about forty yards, and then struck the animal and killed it dead with one blow of his fist! (We might offer the above—which we may say we don't think so unreasonable as some will at first sight suppose—as a special encouragement yet to Johnny Heenan, as against Morrissey. If such things can be done, by human training and muscular energy, even that miraculous endurance and passiveness that won the fight at Long Point, might yet be overcome). This same Milo was six times crowned at the Olympian Games, for his enormous feats of strength, agility and endurance— for all those faculties went together; but the greatest of his points was strength. He was one of the disciples of Pythagoras; and to that same strength the master himself, and several others, owed their lives—for once, in school, the supports under the roof giving way, Milo uplifted the whole of the upper works, giving the philosopher and the rest time to escape, and others a chance to secure the roof from precipitate fall.

Milo was celebrated for such feats as pulling up a respectable-sized tree by the roots—and similar interesting little amusements. We would like the reader, at the same time, to take notice of what we said about this "muscle man" being a student, and doubtless a favorite one, of one of the most celebrated philosophers of antiquity—for then the pursuit of the means toward a superb and mighty-sinewed body was not considered anything else than appropriately joined with the most elevating and refining studies of the intellect.

Augustus Eleventh, a king of Poland, could roll up a silver plate, like a sheet of paper, and twist the strongest horseshoe asunder. We suppose many of our readers must have seen men in the shows who could break quite large-sized stones with a blow of the fist; at any rate we have several times seen such men, and satisfied ourselves that there was no humbug in it. We may, perhaps, as well add to this casual list, a mention of some of the blows given in the Morrissey and Heenan fight—two or three of those blows are said, by old visitors to the prize-ring, here and in England, to have been the heaviest they ever saw given. They would have, without doubt, been certain death to any man not prepared for them by that condition of perfect training which the combatants had both undergone for four months before fighting.

(Four months is no time at all—better say four years; for when the time is small, the injurious fatigue of crowding so much into so small a space, destroys and reacts upon itself. Training ought not to be that hurried and hateful thing it is generally made, on account of these forced reasons, but rather a pleasant, acceptable, gradual, and every way welcomed season of a man's life.)

We were reading, the other day, in a book of travels in Asia that a Hindu runner will run not only all day long, but day after day, by the side of a European traveling on horseback — enduring the travel much better than the horse, or the rider of the horse. Habit, and a certain agility and litheness of body, which seem to be characteristic of the Hindu, make the endurances of these runners among the most remarkable illustrations known of the muscular power of the human body. Indeed, from what we have heard about them, it would seem as if all the running and walking feats we ever have here in America were mere child's play to what is constantly done in India; and that even our famed performances of "walking a thousand miles in a thousand hours," are nothing at all to blow about considering what is common over there.

So much is done by the imperceptible effects of education.

A Turkish porter, for instance, will trot at a rapid pace, carrying a weight of six hundred pounds. You "muscle men" of New York! You will have to improve yourselves considerably yet, we are thinking.

Probably the best and truest average test of muscular endurance and power exists in the locomotive organs, and in their performances. Walking is nature's great physical energy—and, in some form or other, after all, includes the whole expression of life, the passions, and the out-showing of active beauty. Well did the old Greeks, in their highest and most refined games, concentrate their training, and the main interest and fruit of the same, to the point of producing the swiftest and longest-continued locomotion; for they knew, what it is time we should know, that all that goes to make up the heroic physique, and its elements and powers, out of which the other kinds of perfect-bodied men branch and develop themselves—all the stuff of those elements and powers is to be found in the best runners. In other words, there can be no grand physique, for anything, unless it stand well on its legs, and have great locomotive strength and endurance. Make a note of this, reader, and commence regular habits of walking—not forgetting other means of attention to the health, ease, and improvement of the feet, ankles, knees, and all the lower muscles.

The ease of the feet and legs, and their freedom from many of the nonsensical and hurtful environments of modern fashion, are to be insisted on, to begin with. Most of the usual fashionable boots and shoes which neither favor comfort, nor health, nor the ease of walking, are to be discarded. In favorable weather, the shoe now specially worn by the base-ball players would be a very good improvement to be introduced for general use. It should be carefully selected to the shape of the foot, or, better still, made from lasts modeled to the exact shape of the wearer's feet, (as all boots should be.) In a matter of such consequence as ease and pleasure of walking, these things are of serious weight, and cannot be overlooked. Of course, fashion must stand one side, if we are going to enter into the spirit of the thing seriously; no man can serve the two masters, of frivolous fashion and the attainment of robust health and physique, at the same time. You will have to stand out a little; but, like the first shock of entering a swimming-bath, it only needs a little determination at first, and the thing is done.

The daily bathing of the feet in cold water, we have before spoken of. This practice should never be intermitted. The feet, legs, thighs, etc., should also be subjected to the friction of a stiff bristle brush—just the same as the upper limbs. The clothing of the feet is of importance; clean cotton socks in summer, and woolen in winter, carefully selected as to the size. These are little things, but on such little things much depends—yes, even the greatest results depend. And it is, perhaps, to be noted, that many a man who is mighty careful of his outside apparel—his visible coat, vest, neck cloth, jewelry, etc., is habitually careless of the fixings and condition of his feet. Most of the unpleasantness from cold feet, under which many suffer, would also, by following our precepts, be obviated. In this connection, we desire to enter our protest against the use—already too prevalent, and getting more and more so—of the India-rubber shoe; it is a bad article, obstructing the perspiration, and in many ways injuring the feet. There is nothing better for this weather than good leather boots—the feet being, besides, well protected by fresh woolen stockings.

We recommend dancing, as worthy of attention, in a different manner from what use is generally made of that amusement; namely, as capable of being made a great help to develop the flexibility and strength of the hips, knees, muscles of the calf, ankles, and feet. Dancing, on true principles, would have ultimate reference to that, and would then, as an inevitable result, bring grace of movement along with it. There is no reason why, in a good gymnasium, the art of dancing should not also be included, with the intents and purposes we speak of.

WE HAVE BEFORE alluded to the necessity of conforming to all propositions of reform, in manly physique or anything else, as far as possible to the habits and institutions of the day—in conforming to the employments, the common hours of work, and, to some extent, even the prejudices of the people. It is therefore best for those who would follow our advice, in the matter of training, to do so without making any "blow" about it, or setting themselves up in opposition to the right of others to pursue their course also—and likewise without any special vaunts of superior judgment and wisdom. The true trainer is generally known by his quietness and serenity, and never by putting on airs; and the trained man should copy him in these respects.

Besides, after all, in modern society, especially here in America, there is such diversity of taste, and so large an infusion, (getting larger and larger every day) of what we believe the philosophers call "individuality," that a person having any disposition to follow our rules, no matter in what situation of life he may be, or where he may live, can, in the main, do so, without serious impediment or annoyance, so long as he is quiet and self-possessed about it. In all the habitudes of diet and exercise, it is to be considered sufficient if the subject can obey them in the long run, without minding special little interruptions of a meal or so, or of a day or part of a day, which will sometimes be unavoidably forced upon him. The vigor and tone of the manly frame, (as before remarked) are the result of the average course of life, for months, and years, and, in general, need not be seriously disturbed by a casual omission. For all this, which we say by way of consolation for the offences which must come, let the reader understand that our rules are intended to be as consistently and faithfully adhered to as possible—the omissions never without danger.

HEALTH OR DISEASE FOLLOW REGULAR LAWS

It is too generally taken for granted that the formation and preservation of manly strength, and of all those points that conduce to longevity, are the result of accidents, hap-hazard chances, "luck." We wish distinctly to impress it upon the reader that, speaking in general terms, there is no hap-hazard or luck about the matter. In the case of brute animals, all that is necessary is to follow the natural instincts—and, in their case, health is preserved by the perpetual surroundings of the open air, and by the absence of artificial preparations of food. But man, in an artificial life, has come under the control of his reason, judgment, and calculation—with frequent self-denials. We all live surrounded by these artificial circumstances—many of them unfavorable to health and condition. The important object to be gained is, to form the habit of considering these things with reference to their

101

results on the physique—and not any longer accepting them indifferently whenever placed in the midst of them, whether injurious or no.

We repeat it, health and manly strength are under the control of regular and simple laws, and will surely follow the adoption of the means which we have jotted down in the foregoing articles. Indeed, we have often thought, without elaborate study of these laws of health, the desired result might be almost always attained by a little exercise of common sense on the part of him who realized the needlessness and evil of a weak and impure body, and the sure way of retrieving it.

BAD BLOOD

In the shortest way of stating it the cause of disease is bad blood—often hereditary, more often from persistence in bad habits. The object of training is, it may also be stated, to simply purify and invigorate the blood—and when that result is attained, to keep it so.

When we look over the long lists of maladies making such a terrible catalogue, with new additions every year, one is ready to be discouraged, from any attempt at renovation and the establishment of a better order of things—especially, when the doctor's books are studied, with all their formidable arrays of technical terms, (and technical nonsense we were going to add—but that is not in the innocent words, only in the narrowness and short-sight of too many who claim the name of physician.) The discouragement we allude to will be greatly obviated by discarding nineteen-twentieths of the confusing influence of mere names, and looking at this matter of health and disease in the plain bearing of general facts. After that, the particulars may be studied with as much detail as anyone will.

Certain habits, be it definitely understood, invariably produce bad blood and a lowered tone of the system—if continued long enough, ending in what is generally called "a ruined constitution."

How many young men there are in New York, and all our great American cities, who, just for a transient indulgence in a few questionable "pleasures," are thus destroying the priceless treasure of their manhood, strength and virility.

102

There is, (to make a primitive statement of the matter) always so much latent possibility of disease in a man's body—as it were sleeping there, ready to be waked up at any time into powerful and destructive action. So long as the system is kept in good order by healthy observances, there is no trouble from these latent germs; but all forms of dissipation and violations of natural law arouse them and cause them to come rapidly forward. Then fevers, rheumatism, colds, consumption, inflammation, or some other of the scourges—generally looked upon, in the most ignorant manner, as accidental results! Of course, to one who has caught the least portion of the spirit of our theory of training, this error, at least, has become exploded—and he will look on all health and all illness as a play of sensible cause and effect, just as much as building a house, or pulling it down again.

THE THROAT

From various reasons, at the present time, (gradually accumulating in strength and frequency for the last fifty years) a very large proportion of the violations of the laws of health have concentrated in their results in the throat. To our mind the following are some of the leading causes: Feeble and scrofulous parentage, precocious youthful indulgences and passions, a too various and too artificial diet, distilled liquors, syphilitic taint, sedentary employments, continual breathing of stale air, the use of drugs and medicines, etc.. More than half the diseases of the throat come from bad digestion, or no digestion, producing bad blood—in other words come from the stomach. Have you any one of the numerous forms of throat affection? To modify it, perhaps entirely cure it, here is your first course of remedy: discard three-quarters of the varied and unwholesome articles which you have been in the habit of eating, especially for dinner and supper. Make your principal meal, as often as possible, on a slice of beef or mutton, cooked rare, without grease—avoiding every other dish, with scrupulous self-denial. Sup lightly, drink nothing but water, and breathe as much fresh air, winter and summer, as possible. Keep the feet well protected, and use them daily in exercise.

The beard is a great sanitary protection to the throat—for purposes of health it should always be worn, just as much as the hair of the head should be. Think what would be the result if the hair of the head should be carefully scraped off three or four times a week with the razor! Of course, the additional aches, neuralgias, colds, etc., would be immense. Well, it is just as bad with removing the natural protection of the neck; for nature indicates the necessity of that covering there, for full and sufficient reasons.

Of the throat, it may, perhaps, as well be added that its health and strength are doubtless aided by forming the habit of throwing the voice out from it, and not from the mouth only, as many do. The best Italian singers, it will be noticed, have that utterance—sending out the sound from the back of the mouth; in most of the New England states the bad-sounding and unwholesome practice of speaking through the front of the mouth only, and through the nose as much as the mouth, is very prevalent.

We have said that the bad condition of the general health ends and shows itself, in many cases, in these throat-diseases spoken of. We are not sure but this is almost invariably the case; for we have noticed that persons with the aforesaid throat-diseases are those whose blood is bad, either clogged with the thick and morbid consequences of gluttony and inebriate habits, or else the thin and watery blood of persons whose food does not assimilate to and nourish the system. Because what is there in the throat itself, the windpipe, (trachea) or the bronchial tubes, (two continuations forking down from the trachea, and leading into the lungs)—what is there in these, or their ramifications, to become diseased except from bad blood? Medicines, for any of the ailments of the throat will of course be ordered by the ordinary physician, and may give temporary relief—but the only effectual medicine lies in the entire purification and renovation of the life of the body, the blood, after the spirit of the hints we have jotted down in our fore- going articles. It must be borne in mind also, that one of the greatest dangers of all throat-diseases is that they lead to the last and most dreaded result of all bad blood, consumption,—lungs honey- combed and consumed—the destruction of the power to vivify the blood. Much is said in books, newspapers, schools of medicines, and among the doctors, over the question, can consumption be cured? When the evil processes have gone on long enough to destroy a lung, or a great portion of the lung, it is vain to think of restoring the lost member, of course; and, in most cases, the best that can be done is to stave off the final dissolution as long as possible. But the true statement to put before the people is that which makes them realize what causes consumption, and all other serious diseases of the lungs, throat, and the like. It is absurd to confuse the plain popular mind with volleys of technical terms, doctor's Latin, etc.; the simple underlying truths should be set forth in common English and made to come home to the experience and understanding of every one.

VIRTUE OF OUT-DOORS, AND A STIRRING LIFE

What is the reason that a voyage to sea, or a journey to California, or off for months and months in a wild country, perhaps exposed to many unusual hardships and privations, half-starved, or fed on what, under ordinary circumstances, would prove unwholesome food—what is the reason, we say, that this often proves the means of re-establishing the health previously in decay, or quite given up? The actual reason of any case necessitates knowledge of the special particulars of that case; for there are hardly any two that are precisely alike (which proves the folly of the usual pretensions of the cure-all medicines).

Generally speaking there is that virtue in the open air, and a stirring life therein, that has more effect than any or all the prescriptions that go forth from the apothecary's shop. Hunters, raftsmen, lumbermen, and all those whose employments are away from the close life and dissipation of cities—what specimens of manly strength and beauty they frequently are! We throw out this sort of hint, in our usual rapid way, for you, reader, to cogitate upon, and draw the moral yourself.

Not that we wish to see you take to the woods or rivers—for we think you can attain all the desired results without leaving your home in the city, if you choose to stay here. But to hint that, so long as you give up your own self-control and allow yourself to be a victim to all these pestiferous little gratifications that are offered to you in the city, so long will you present a marked contrast to the noble physique of the lumberman and hunter.

Often, a complete change of scene, associations, companionship, habits, etc., is the best thing that can be done for a man's health, (and the change is perhaps beneficial to a further extent in his morals, knowledge, etc.) If you are "in a bad way" from associations, etc., wisdom and courage both indicate to you to pull up stakes and leave for a new spot—careful there to begin aright, and persevere with energy. This advice is of more necessity than might be supposed. There are thousands of young men now in New York, and in all American cities, who go on year after year, slaves of habits they know to be bad, but pressing close and helpless upon them, because they are also the habits of their friends and intimate companions. To such, our counsel is, Up and away!

COLD-WEATHER

The winter has now set in, and some remarks appropriate to it may not be amiss. In America, where the close stove [Cast-iron stove] is used everywhere, much injury to health results therefrom, in consequence of the frequent and sudden changes of temperature, vibrating every hour or two between the bitter cold of the outdoor air and the stifling heat of an unventilated room, warmed by a red hot coal fire. Neither the throat nor lungs can stand such abrupt changes, continued month after month, and winter after winter. Neuralgia, aching joints, colds, coughs, etc., joined with inflammations and fevers, and great derangements of the stomach and bowels, are among the liabilities of health at the commencement of winter; for a change in the temperature "strikes in" where the subject has bad stuff in him, and stirs it up to action, one way or another. As to general habits, especially of diet, we can but refer the reader to our former articles, confident that they will apply to a greater or less extent to every case that can be devised. We would, however, make a few remarks upon dress, as appropriate for the winter. Many persons dress too much in winter for their own good—too much for the very purpose of keeping warm. Excess of clothing is really one of the most frequent causes of that tender sensitiveness to cold, which is so annoying in our climate, resulting in a morbidly sensitive skin, and thence great suffering from all those exposures to cold air, which, of course, in our climate, are almost unavoidable.

The best rule is, instead of putting on all the clothing one can stand, to dress as lightly as is consistent with comfort, at the same time affording all parts of the body their requisite protection.

The most prevalent error, of course, is too little protection about the feet, and too much about the head and neck. Since shaving has come in practice, (it ought to be scouted entirely from all northern countries) and since heavy mufflers, neck-winders, shawls, etc., have got to be generally used, all sorts of head and throat distempers have multiplied a hundred-fold. A physician of our acquaintance once informed us that he had known several cases of liability to throat-inflammation entirely cured by simply washing the neck regularly every morning, the year round, in cool water, and dispensing with all thick "comforters" in winter, with nothing but a light and loose handkerchief, leaving the throat open.

We have spoken before of the morning ablutions—we mean the cool bath for the whole body. No doubt many of our readers will start back in dismay from such a proposition this whether; yet this is what we seriously mean. Not, be it well understood, for the feeble, the puny, the invalid, but for the robust, the young, and the sound only. This, cautiously begun, and by degrees formed into a habit, will so invigorate the whole surface as to make one indifferent during the day to the severest cold, and enjoy comfort in it, while others are chilly and shivering.

Then, after all is said about dress and other outside observances, we revert back to our theory of the other final under stratum of warmth, health, comfort, and any other bodily perfection, viz., good blood—all sound inside. "The life-principle within," somebody has wisely observed, "is our main protection against the elements without." Yes, and against all the bodily changes, and the liabilities to disease. The quality of the blood and the state of its circulation— if these are amiss, no care or amount of dress will keep a man warm or comfortable. They have to do with the condition of the skin, which, of course, is nothing in itself, but only a register or medium, to act between the "life principle" inside the body and the elements without.

In walking, these wintry days, we see that the men through our streets have adopted the fashion of carrying themselves with head bent downward, and arms and shoulders tightly drawn in—very much after the mode of the turtle withdrawing its head into its shell. We submit that such is not the habit a man should form for his walking style—but always go with the head erect and breast expanded—always throwing open the play of the great vital organs, inhaling the good air into the throat, lungs and stomach, and giving tone to the whole system thereby.

Another thing; hot drinks of all kinds do more hurt than good in cold weather—there is always a reaction. The morbid habit of drinking excessively, (we include tea, coffee, and water also, just the same) is at any season pernicious to the sound state of the body, and especially so in winter. We advise the reader, if he be ambitious of that kind of a "good time" which is superior to all others, perfect bodily comfort in winter, to follow the old maxim, "keep the feet warm and the head cool," the body evenly and moderately clad, studying all our preceding articles and faithfully observing their directions—continuing on with a couple of others that are to follow, (for we are drawing nigh to the end of our rope)—accustom himself as much as convenient to outdoor exercise—and thus, we assure him, he will, in all likelihood, pass through the winter with a degree of pleasure that will not only more than repay him for his trouble, but will give him new ideas of the capacity of bliss the simple sensation of "feeling well" is able to produce.

CHAPTER 11

IN THE COURSE of reading one of these articles only, we must here remark, en passant, the student of health and a manly physique will by no means be apt to get a fair view of our positions, and of those points that have a bearing on the subject. It is necessary that all the preceding articles of this series should be carefully read also. We have there jotted down, as they presented themselves to our mind, most of the primary rules that are to be followed by him who would achieve a sound and clear-blooded condition of body. We have spoken of health as being the real foundation of all manly beauty, and have done our part toward dissipating the pink-and-white doll theory of masculine good appearance. We have shown that all sickliness is fatal to beauty, and the inference follows, unavoidably, that much of the prevailing taste is morbid and unsound.

Our series is drawing to a close. This article, and one more to follow, finishes them. Disconnected as our mode of writing has been, and intended from the first to be given off-hand and just as the subjects presented themselves to our mind, we are aware that the reader who peruses one article only, will not see the drift of our writing—which we should consider an entire failure if, in a total review of it, we did not find to be compact, effective for the purpose it aims at, and comprehensive. To those of our readers who have seen only partial sections of this series, we can only repeat our charge and wish that they procure the entire series, which, if they take an interest in the subject, will amply repay them, and give them, we are sure, many new and useful items of information.

For these two concluding numbers of our series, we find we have a few more items to give, which we shall proceed to jot down in the same manner as hitherto.

The object of a correspondent, who writes to complain of our series that "the spirit of such articles is to make an entire nation of fighting men," we think we have already answered in a preceding section. If not, we may as well confess that we do not deny the charge, but admit it. We would be quite willing to have the young men of America thoroughly trained to be able to give a good account of themselves in all contests, muscular, military, naval, and otherwise. As to the danger of belligerent habits, why for that we must take chances. We would rather see an occasional "muss," either on a small scale or a large one, than that continual and supple obedience which the opposite tack would be likely to produce.

Another correspondent (for we have had several) objects to our statement of the time that a man ought to be in good condition, and considers it, for general purposes, quite chimerical to expect that a man, in modern times, can last, in robust tone, from his twenty-fourth or fifth to his sixty-fifth year. Very well—our correspondent is of one opinion, and we are of another; that's the difference. We dare say a great many of the views we have expressed will find denials here and there; but what would be worth those statements that only repeat what is already so well known that it would meet a ready assent everywhere? We do not think, indeed, upon referring to our already written articles, that we have given sufficient prominence to the subject of middle-age, in all its bearings, and with reference to the flush condition of health, strength, etc., which belongs to it. We consider that the same condition and qualities, in a fitly trained man, may well be expected to advance far into the confines of what is generally termed old age. The ancients were full of the examples of this, and we see occasionally an intimation of it in modern fanciful writing.

MIDDLE AND OLD AGE

Somebody who writes in the metaphorical style of the litterateurs of a century and a half ago, encloses some very useful wisdom in the following paragraph:

From forty to sixty a man who has properly regulated himself may be considered as in the prime of life. His matured strength of constitution renders him almost impervious to the attacks of disease, and experience has given his judgment the soundness of almost infallibility. His mind is resolute, firm and equal; all his functions are in the highest order; he assumes the mastery over business; builds up a competence on the foundation he has formed in early manhood,

110

and passes through a period of life attended by many gratifications. Having gone a year or two past sixty, he arrives at a critical period in the road of existence; the river of death flows before him, and he remains at a stand-still. But athwart this river is a viaduct, called "The Turn of Life," which, if crossed in safety, leads to the valleys of "Old Age," round which the river winds, and then flows beyond without a boat or causeway to effect its passage. The bridge is, however, constructed of fragile materials, and it depends upon how it is trodden whether it bend or break. Gout, apoplexy, and other bad characters are also in the vicinity to waylay the traveler and thrust him from the pass; but let him gird up his loins, and provide himself with a fitting staff, and he may trudge on in safety, with perfect composure.

Indeed, a very amusing and interesting volume might be written on the theme the above paragraph treats of, in the style of Bunyan's "Pilgrim's Progress." It would come home as close to the feelings and experience of people as anything in that celebrated work—substituting the physical for the moral and spiritual, which latter Bunyan has treated with such marvelous ingenuity and power.

The periods of middle and old age are perhaps the finest, in some of the most important respects, through life. We dwell upon this the more, because we notice that too many of the tendencies of American city life so destroy the chances for this middle and old perfection, that it seems to have gone out of mind. No one seems to understand that there is attainable a high flush condition of stamina, strength, vigor, personality, clearness and manly beauty and love-power, thoroughly sustained many years, in perfect specimens of trained health, through middle and old age, towering in its ripeness and completeness, till it rivals and fully equals the best and handsomest specimens of early manhood—and indeed transcends them!

The mind of one familiar with antique models at once turns to the palmy ages of Greek art, and of its Roman copyists. All the grandest characters who appear in it are middle aged or old men—and they rise into colossal proportions. No matter what the field—war, adventure, love, or what not—they are the principal figures in the foreground, or eminent above the mass.

But how can we expect specimens of perfect physique, these

years, to rival the ancient ones, unless the models are more steadily present- ed before us? As things are, all the ambition of the young is turned in intellectual channels—to a monstrous development of the mind, and of what is called "knowledge."

TOO MUCH BRAIN ACTION AND FRETTING

In addition to what we have already said in preceding articles, it seems necessary for us, as a counterbalance, to add a few further remarks on this part of the subject. It is indisputable that many lives are prematurely sacrificed by a too restless intellect and brain—the action thereof literally rushing a man into his grave. All through America, especially North and East, not only among the writers, lawyers, editors, preachers, etc., but through the ranks of the masses, there is altogether too much brain action, sapping the foundation of life, and of the enjoyment of life. The intellect is too restless. The parent bequeaths the tendency to the child—and he, when grown up, has it in increased force. Some direct it toward money-making, others to religion, and so on. It eats into the whole temperament, and produces reaction; then for fits of "the blues," and an   unhappy life.

The remedy lies with the person himself. He must let up on his brain and thought-power, and form more salutary and reasonable habits—which, by-the-way, are formed astonishingly soon, if once sternly resolved upon, and the practice commenced in earnest. The homely advice to "take things easy," applies with particular force to this sort of persons. Most of the ills they labor under, and the dispensations they dread, are imaginary; at any rate, imagination distorts them, and magnifies them out of all proportion. A little calmness and coolness puts to flight three-fourths of the evils of their lives.

But the mere fact of intense mental action is itself a misfortune. We repeat again, how much it is to be regretted that, in the prevailing theories of education, the desire to make young persons prodigies of learning, statistics, science, and mental brilliancy, have gone so far in what we are clear is a very dangerous and unwholesome direction—that is, if manly health and happiness are, as they are, first to be considered in a boy's and young man's life. These hints should be more thoroughly accepted by parents and teachers, and acted upon in families and schools.

By undue action, development and concentration, the brain begets upon the system and character a high state of excitability and inflammation often resulting in later life, and sometimes in middle age, in the condition of softening of the brain. It is a terribly malady, not so much for its amount of suffering as for the pitiable condition to which it reduces the most colossal intellect. Sir Walter Scott, Daniel Webster, Dean Swift, and hundreds of persons of lesser note, are instances of the play of cause and effect resulting in this fearful disease, which has various phases, but is of one general type. Literary men, and persons in the excitement of political life, are especially liable to it, from the uncertain nature of their employment and popularity, the strain upon the brain-power, and probably also from the cares and jealousies that are forever multiplying among them, aggravated no doubt by their generally reckless habits, and irritable tempers; and besides from something inherent in the nature of their occupation, waiting upon the public. To them, too, the only salvation is in rising superior to all such petty fears and bickering—otherwise they are at any time liable to the consequences of which we have just given the most signal examples.

And yet, as before intimated, a diseased brain, and a sadly inflamed state of the nervous system, are by no means confined to literary men. We Americans altogether, all classes, think too much, and too morbidly, —brood, meditate, become sickly with our own pallid fancies, allowing them to swarm upon us by night and by day. It will, of course, sound strange in the ears of many to say so, but we are fain to proclaim over and over again, in our loudest and most emphatic tones, we are too intellectual a race. To the brain parts of our structure we draw off much that should be devoted to the body, the muscles—neglecting what all men first require, to be fine animals. We suppose we shall excite some disdain by such remarks, but they include undoubted truths necessary to be told.

Not that calm and wholesome brain-action, tempered with regular exercise and development of the body, is meant to be called injurious. On the contrary, that no doubt tends to longevity, and is consistent with the best health, and is perhaps a part of it—as it is the crowning glory of a rational being, and endows the finest condition of the body with grace and beauty, otherwise lacking.

No; duly tempered mental labor is justified in the lives of its votaries in all ages. Plato lived to be 81 years of age, Diogenes 90, Democritus 100, Zeno 102, and indeed all the most celebrated philosophers and poets of ancient times seem to have been long-lived, and to have produced their most famous works in old age. In more modern times Newton attains the age of 84, Harvey that of 88, Franklin 84, Noah Webster 85, and so on. In France, a statistician, selecting at random one hundred and fifty scientific and literary men, one half from the Academy of Sciences, the other half from that of Belles Lettres, found the average age of life attained by them to be the ripe age of 70 years. Of the ancient poets and philosophers, it is always worthy of remembrance that some of the greatest of them are as much celebrated for their physical strength and beauty as for their mental. Pythagoras, the father and master, was of large, imposing and elegantly shaped body; he often entered the arena and contended with the athletes for the prizes in running, leaping, fighting, etc., and won them too! We might ask our modern puny and dandy tribes of literary men to make a note of such facts.

CITY LIFE

The great requisites of health being good air, proper food, and appropriate exercise, the two latter of course can be as well accomplished in the city as country—leaving the matter of pure air as the only doubtful point. And why could we not have a good atmosphere in the city? The reader, accustomed to the prevailing state of things, may think this is a very unreasonable question, and yet we utter it in all seriousness. Because we think a clear and deeply based popular appreciation of the truth, with all its play of causes and effects, relating to this point, would almost certainly in the end lead to the means of having the kind of atmosphere we speak of.

The means of accomplishing this most desirable result consist of a perfect system of sewerage, in which no part or section of the city whatever shall be neglected—and in an organized plan, whose details should be overseen by the police, for gathering and carrying away daily all the garbage and refuse of the city; and these details should be joined with a rigid and perpetual sanitary inspection of every block in the city, every street, every alley, every yard. But could this be done? Of course it could be done; and the day will arrive when it will be done. Then the airs of our streets, instead of being reeking and pestiferous during the hot season, will not offend the most delicate nostrils.

There is, however, much in cities; it remains to be said, which is not sufficiently appreciated as offering great advantages for health. The markets, with their luxuries, afford their selection from a list of simple articles, to him who realizes the importance of attaining a fine physique, primarily through the stomach, the careful choice of his daily aliment. This is no trifling advantage, and it is one which is often deficient in the country; there the prevailing food is apt to be salt meat, vegetables, etc., which (the truth may as well be told) are by no means the articles most favorable to produce a race of clear-blooded and sound-conditioned men. The often-mentioned superiority of the country receives a great drawback on this account. And with respect to the matter of good air, it is to be recollected that it is of serious importance only through the three or four hot months of the year. We do not intend to deprecate its vital bearings upon health, but are not willing to have the truth overstated, or made worse than it is. During the fall, winter and spring, most of our cities are as healthy as any country place. Nor let it be forgotten that a very large proportion of country places are pervaded with an atmosphere more or less bad and unwholesome. Exhalations and vapors rise and spread around, often in neighborhoods where everything looks fair and inviting to the eye. The frame-racking and blood-thinning disease of fever and ague, which annually ruins its tens of thousands of men, is one of the results of country air. In general terms, it may be stated that the rude forms and florid complexions of healthy specimens of country life, are to be attributed to their more natural hours, early rising, exercise, open air, and their being less under the influence of the artificial habits and overtaxed mentality which mark the life of the citizen. If citizens would only make a reasonable use of their many priceless advantages, knock off some of their artificial habits, and take   daily exercise, avoiding all dissipations, they would soon show not only equally noble specimens of health with the country, but superior to them.

CHAPTER 12

CAN WE THEN HAVE AS FINE A RACE OF MEN IN MODERN ARTIFICIAL LIFE, AS IN RUDER AGES?

ARE NOT THE present races of men, through the civilized world, far less hardy and sound, less perfect as specimens of noble physique, than they were one hundred, two hundred, and three hundred years ago? We much fear that this question will have to be answered in the affirmative. We have heard it stoutly maintained that the present races are as physically perfect as any previous ones; but our own opinion is that the prevalence of a far more artificial life, and the occupation of such myriads of men, these times, in close factories, and all kinds of indoor work, joined with other causes, (among which may be specified the frightful adulteration of most of the grocery articles of food), have had a deleterious effect on the general health, in comparison with what, according to all accounts, must have been presented by former times.

Is this inevitable? That is the most important question. Can we not have the principal advantages of modern civilization, with their factories, vast ranks of employees, and all the grand accompaniments of great cities, without having also a deteriorated race of men? We are clear enough that this latter is not the necessary result; but that, in easy accord with modern forms, with factories, the life of cities, and all the modern requirements and usages, these may be conformed to, and still, under training and physiological laws, the health kept robust, and a noble physique developed. We believe that reason, resolution, and training, are equal to all resolutions and emergencies. But it is necessary that working men, with the rest, should understand, without softening the matter that their best salvation depends upon their entering upon, and a persistent adherence in, a rigid course of training and habits of health. With that made general, the difference between the hardy life of old times, and our artificial forms of life, would disappear—and a fine race of men be produced.

COULD THERE BE AN ENTIRE NATION OF VIGOROUS AND BEAUTIFUL MEN?

We think it not too much to demand that not only the theories of public education, but that the municipal government, in appropriate ways, should recognize and favor manly training, so conducive to the public health, and to filling the land with a superior and every way better race of men. The legislative authorities have long recognized the propriety of caring for the intellectual development of the young; but we believe, and think we have advanced reasons to prove, not only that the physical stands first in order, and should take precedence of the other, but that the other cannot be carried on, with any degree of profit and safety, except it be combined with the training and strengthening of a fine physique, and founded upon it.

We are not prepared to say exactly in what way the recognition and support of the authorities should be bestowed. It is enough at present to broach the matter, giving a few of the reasons that have a bearing upon it—and then leaving the case to work out its consequences.

As to the schools, we have long been of opinion that no school should be established, in city or country, without its training department, its gymnasium, where health, vigor, cleanliness, activity, and the simple and broad laws of physiology, are exemplified for the young. We do not mean merely places of exercise, but of training in its full sense, with reference to the establishment of good habits of diet, self-denial, chastity, temperance, etc., or of inculcating the knowledge of them, at any rate, so that they may be generally diffused. We are encouraged to hope that these articles, among many means now at work, may help towards producing that most desirable result.

To us it is quite certain that, by right observances, an entire nation of men may be vigorous and beautiful—that is, that they will form the rule, and be common, while feebleness and bad looks will be the exception. What a result this would be! As it is, even with all their excesses, their dyspepsia, their abuse and overtasking of the brain, the Americans are undoubtedly the handsomest men, as a race, now upon the earth. What would they be with general sound health, and perfect physiques?

STRENGTH OF FUTURE AMERICANS

It is a favorite theory of ours that the generations of men, in America, have yet to witness the immense perfection of physical strength that is to be attained, and to become quite general—common enough, at any rate, not to excite the remarks it now does, or serve as a wonder, a monstrosity. We have in our time seen some pretty tall specimens of strength, among the rest a Belgian, who was exhibited a few years ago in New York, named J. A. Bihin. He could lift from the ground, with his hands, eight hundred pounds, and straighten his back, when stooping, under a weight of two tons. His size, however, was the most formidable part of him. He was seven feet and a half in height; he measured fifty inches round the chest, twenty-eight inches round the thigh, and twenty-two inches round the calf of the leg—and his weight was three hundred and twenty pounds. He was no monstrosity, but was of symmetrical form throughout.

But very great strength may reside in persons of ordinary general size, and is often to be found there. Good parentage is a great thing; but training, and proper and systematic exercise, is also capable of bringing out strength to a very great degree, in those who have not inherited it.

As an illustration of the power of man's endurance, it is well known that a properly trained pedestrian can tire out a horse, (it is said any horse) on a pull sufficiently long to tax the powers of each to the utmost. In oriental countries, the performances of the Indian footmen and runners, stage after stage, day after day, are almost incredible. There seems to be no tire to the soles of their feet. They are brought up to it from their earliest youth, and so get to have unsurpassed wind and bottom. All this, too, on a simple sustenance of rice and milk, dried fruits, and the like—as, to many of them, a meat diet is unknown.

119

MORE ABOUT EATING AND DRINKING

Probably the last as well as the first thing to be mentioned, and attended to, for one who considers the subject of health, and of putting himself in systematic training for its conditions, is that of diet—what he may eat and drink, and what he must avoid. Here will generally be the hardest tug of all. Everybody loves good living; and the ingenuity of modern cookery has created so many dishes to satisfy that love, that few will, at first, be willing to apply that stern check on their appetites which is necessary. It needs to be stated, however, with entire candor, that whoso wants a fine physique, continued through middle age, and carried on to old age, must fulfill this part of the conditions, or the rest will be of no avail. Most of the artificial luxuries, solid and liquid, must be cut off. Soups, pastry, fat, onions, gravies, puddings, sauces, brandy, gin, coffee, jellies, may be specified, not as by any means comprising the whole list of contraband articles, but as heading the list; nor must we forget to put in cigars and tobacco. It is useless to make a stand on these things. To the young man who sets out with the will to accomplish the end we have been placing before him, the result must reward him for his denial of these and similar gratifications.

Have greater care, very much greater care, in the choice of articles used for your food, and also in the manner of their being cooked. It is no discredit to a man, young or old, for him to show that he is jealous of his condition, and that he is determined to use the means which will preserve that condition.

What then may be eaten? If you want to know what is best to a hearty man, who takes plenty of exercise and fresh air, and don't want any pimples on his face or body, we will answer, (perhaps very much to your astonishment) a simple diet of rare-cooked beef, seasoned with a little salt, and accompanied with stale bread or sea-biscuit. Mutton, if lean and tender, is also commendable. Pork should not be eaten. Butter, pepper, catsup, oil, and most of the "dressings," must also be eschewed. Lobster and chicken salad, cabbage, cucumbers, and even potatoes, are to be turned away from. Salted meats are not to be partaken of either; and salt itself, as a seasoning, is to be used as sparingly as possible. There is quite a great popular error we will mention here, on the use of salt for food. It by no means has the merit that is generally attributed to it; but, on the contrary, if used to excess, causes a very vicious state of the blood. Salt is a mineral, and it is not solved in the juices of the body.

With early rising and "taking an airing," there will be no need of an appetite for breakfast, which, under the rules we have stated, may be pretty fully indulged in. The same as to dinner; the supper, which must not be at a late hour, we would recommend always to be light— occasionally making this meal to consist of fruit, either fresh, during the middle and latter part of the summer—and of stewed fruit during the winter and spring. As to a hearty supper of rich viands, that must be forborne on all occasions—especially by those who have to use the vocal organs in public; speakers, singers, actors, preachers, etc. For it is a well-settled fact that the voice is seriously injured by such suppers, and the "wind" (as it is called in sporting phrase) gradually weakened and broken up. If the singer or public speaker only knew how incomparably superior his voice would become, and how steady and reliable on all occasions, under the rigid physiological habitudes we have been laying down, he would need no further persuasion from us to initiate and persevere in these rules, especially as regards diet. It is to be understood that there is an intimate analogy between many parts of the training necessary for athletic physical performances, and that necessary for a first-class vocalist.

Of the drink, the same stern system of abstinence is to be observed. Dr. Forsyth, a great training authority among "the fancy" on the other side of the Atlantic, says: "Medically speaking, as regards drink, we should say that water would be the best liquor in training. But it is never given alone in modern times, as it is thought to be a weakening diluent. The ancient athletes, however, were allowed nothing but water, or a sort of thick and sweet wine. The drink preferred by modern English trainers, for the ring, is good old malt liquor, in bottles, and as mild as possible, without any perceptible tartness of harshness, (this is for the English climate, however, not American, which is different.) Those who do not like malt liquor, particularly for breakfast, (they never have coffee or tea) are allowed by the trainers a small quantity of wine or water. Cool tea is sometimes permitted, but this reluctantly, as it is not considered strengthening. Hot, or even warm liquor, of any kind, is considered as enervating and weakening to the tone of the system, and is not given—except warm gruel or beef tea, when taking physic. By the best English trainers, no spirits, (brandy, gin, etc.) are ever permitted, not even with water, at any time, or under any pretense; if used, it is always against their serious protest. No milk is allowed either, as, if creamy and rich, it is too fattening and plethoric. No drink is permitted, before meals, unless there be distressing thirst."

Among the English, Scotch and Irish trainers, quite a favorite refreshment to be given their men is a "gruel," a compound of oat meal, water and salt. This is carefully prepared, quite a large quantity, in a pitcher, and it is free to the man in training, at any hour, day or night, at exercise or between meals—with no other restriction than the man's own appetite. We have heard so much of oatmeal, and of the potent sanitary results of using it as an ailment, that we confess we are curious to see it introduced and tried in America. Would it not make a very cheap, simple, and agreeable addition to the variety of our food here? Cannot some agriculturalist or food speculator take the hint?

Among the additional rules that may be mentioned with regard to eating, are such as follow:

- Make the principal part of your meal always of one dish.
- Chew the food well, and do not eat fast.
- Wait until you feel a good appetite before eating—even if the regular hour for a meal has arrived.
- We have spoken against the use of the potato. It still remains to be said that if it agrees with you, and you are fond of it, it may be used; it is best properly boiled, at the morning meal. Do not partake of it, however, except in moderation.
- Drink very sparingly at each meal; better still not at all—only between meals, when thirsty.

Any article craved by the appetite, and not of essential importance to be prohibited, may be allowed in moderation. This permission, however, does not extend to spirituous liquors.

In general terms, avoid what disagrees with you; for there are, to every individual case, certain rules which apply to it alone. Study these, as they relate to your own case.

There are even cases where a vegetarian diet applies. Such persons have an antipathy to eat meat. Of course, to them, it follows that they must eat what their appetite will permit, and what agrees with them.

A cheerful and gay temper during and immediately after meals, is a great help to health.

Never take any violent or strained exercise immediately after a meal.

Our own opinion is, that if things could be so arranged, it would be best to make the heartiest meal in the morning, instead of the middle of the day. This, however, is contrary to modern usage, and would in most cases be inconvenient.

Use no artificial means, "bitters," or any other stimulants, to create a false appetite. If you have none, do not eat till it comes.

Finally, our repeated charge is that all spices, pepper, strong mustard, pickles, pungent preserves, bitters, tobacco, and strong liquor generally, not only injure the stomach by their excessive stimulus and fiery qualities, but the tone of the palate, the taste, by making plain and wholesome food become tasteless. To one, for instance who is used to plastering over his beefsteak with a thick coat of pungent sauce of some kind, mustard or the like, a plain broiled steak, seasoned only with a pinch of salt, would relish poorly indeed. Yet the latter is by far the best for health; and there is no sauce like regular and daily exercise, and fresh air.

A WORD OF ENCOURAGEMENT

What then to persons in a bad condition? After the body has been reduced by illness, and the whole organism racked and wrecked by powerful drugs, as well as prostrating disease; after the energy and endurance of youth and early manhood have passed, and one has become the slave of custom, and has, perhaps, given up the hope of health, is there still a chance remaining for such a man? Even so, we do not promise anything in the style of some of the medicine advertisements, but say that through simple and natural methods, there arises such virtue out of a few plain laws, and following a few sanitary rules, that, in due time, the result will be, in nine cases out of ten, health and comfort.

CONCLUSION

We know very well that we have not gone over the whole field, but that much, very much, might still be mentioned, having a bearing, more or less remote, on manly training and the conditions of strength and a perfect physique. In our off-hand articles, however, we have not so much been induced by the desire to comprehend the whole subject, as to broach it to the reader, and give him a few leading hints, out of which the rest will follow; for he who once gets started, fully awakened to the precious endowment he has in his own body, beyond all other wealth that can be acquired by man, will not cease his interest in the subject, but will go on toward a greater and greater degree of inquiry, knowledge, and perfection.

One great point we would again impress on you reader, (we have before reverted to it) is the fact that your own individual case doubtless has points and circumstances which more or less modify all the general laws, and perhaps call for special ones, for yourself. This is an important consideration in all theories and statements of health.

What we have given has been the general statement—the great highway of manly health, on which all may travel, and must travel; and this is indeed for all. Still there are many little by-ways and lanes leading to particular homes.

Common reason, and such knowledge as we have hastily outlined in the foregoing articles, will clear the way for you in most particulars. Occasionally the advice of an intelligent and conscientious physician may be necessary—and such men are to be found yet. But, generally speaking, the benefit of or medicine or medical advice is very much overrated. Nature's medicines are simple food, nursing, air, rest, cheerful encouragement, and the like. The art of the surgeon is certain and determined—that of the physician is vague, and affords an easy cover to ignorance and quackery. The land is too full of poisonous medicines and incompetent doctors—the less you have to do with them the better.

Our remarks, as we stated in the beginning, are especially intended for young men. If read over with that attention and earnestness which we are sure they deserve, and then followed with faith and manly perseverance, we feel it not too much to say, we can promise that reliable result, the purpose of all, a sound body and the condition of perfect health.

In that condition your whole body and consequently your spirits too, will be elevated to a state by other persons unknown—made clear and light, inwardly and outwardly elastic—made solid, strong, and yet of rapid movement. A singular charm, better than what is called beauty, flickers out of and over your face; a transparency beams in the eyes, both in the iris and the white; you exhibit a new grace in walk, and indeed in all your movements—in the voice, which rings clearer, and has melody, perhaps, for the first time. Few are aware how much a sound condition of the whole organism of the body has to do with the voice.

Not only the looks and movement, but the feelings, undergo a trans- formation. It may almost be said that sorrows and disappointments cease: there is no more borrowing trouble. With perfect health, (and regular agreeable occupation) there are no low spirits, and cannot be. A man realizes the old myth of the poets; he is a god walking the earth. He not only feels new powers in himself—he sees new beauties everywhere. His faculties, his eyesight, his hearing, all acquire superior capacity to give him pleasure. Indeed, merely to move is a pleasure; the play of the limbs in motion is enough. To breathe, to eat and drink the simplest food, out vie the most costly of previous enjoyments.

Many of those beforehand gratifications, especially those of the palate, drink, spirits, fat, grease, coffee, strong spices, pepper, pastry, crust, mixtures, etc., are put aside voluntarily—become distasteful. The appetite is voracious enough, but it demands simple aliment. Those others were vexatious dreams—and now the awakening.

How happily pass the days! A blithe carol bursts from the throat to greet the opening morn. The fresh air is inhaled—exercise spreads the chest—every sinew responds to the call upon it—the whole system seems to laugh with glee. The occupations of the forenoon pass swiftly and cheerfully along; the dinner is eaten with such zest as only perfect health can give—and the remaining hours still continue to furnish, as they arrive, new sources of filling themselves, and affording contentment.

How sweet the evenings! The labors of the day over—whether on a farm, or in the factory, the workshop, the forge or furnace, the ship- yard, or what not—then rest is realized indeed. For who else but such as they, can realize it? It is a luxury almost worth being poor to enjoy. The healthy sleep—the breathing deep and regular—the unbroken and profound repose—the night as it passes soothing and renewing the whole frame. Yes, nature surely keeps her choicest blessings for the slumber of health—and nothing short of that can ever know what true sleep is.

ABOUT WALT WHITMAN

Walter "Walt" Whitman was a poet, essayist and journalist. He was a part of the transition between transcendentalism and realism, and incorporated both views in his works. Among the most influential poets in America, much of his work was deeply controversial when first published.

Whitman was born in the year 1819 at Huntington, Long Island (New York). During his life he worked as a journalist, teacher, government clerk, and was a nurse during the Civil War. Whitman's major work, Leaves of Grass, was first published in 1855 and is an attempt to reach out to the common man in America. He continued expanding and revising it until his death in Camden, New Jersey in 1892.

ABOUT EVAN ROFHEART

Evan Rofheart has been on a "transcendental" spiritual path since he was fifteen years old when he was initiated into the technique of Transcendental Meditation in 1973. He was later made a teacher of TM by Maharishi Mahesh Yogi, (Guru to the Beatles).

In the early 1980s Evan founded Rofheart International Oil, in Houston, Texas, a company and business model which revolutionized the Oil Trading and Oil Brokerage business. After leaving the oil business, Evan founded numerous other businesses; he has sold and leased jet aircraft throughout the world, run a successful restaurant, started and operated a chain of magazine stores in the New York Metropolitan area, and he even spent a few years in the motion picture industry.

By the latter part of the 1990s, after attending Drexel University in Philadelphia, Evan realized his life-long dream of working in architecture; he has successfully designed and managed major projects for film director Steven Spielberg, the gallery owner Larry Gagosian and many other clients in New York's Hamptons.

In 2016 Evan founded Enlightenment Press to make books and publications available through various platforms. Publishing does seem to be in his blood, his mother was the Historical Novelist, Martha Rofheart. He lives in Manhattan, with his three small children.

51975317R00080

Made in the USA
Lexington, KY
12 May 2016